OUT

of

BODY

EXPERIENCES

How to Have
Them and What
to Expect

ROBERT PETERSON

HAMPTON ROADS

Cover art by Radius/SuperStock

Hampton Roads Publishing Company, Inc.
Charlottesville, VA 22906
Distributed by Red Wheel/Weiser, LLC
www.redwheelweiser.com

Sign up for our newsletter and special offers by going to
www.redwheelweiser.com/newsletter/.

ISBN: 978-1-57174-699-3

Library of Congress Cataloging-in-Publication data available
upon request

Printed on acid-free paper in United States of America
MAL
10 9 8 7 6 5 4 3 2 1

Contents

Foreword

This is an interesting book, but much more than that, it's an important one. It deals with something vital to us all: our souls.

A leading national news magazine recently reported that books which deal with the soul or that have the word "soul" in their title have been on the best seller lists a lot in recent years. The tone of the supposedly "objective" report had that faint ring of cynicism we've come to associate with media today through the implied question of: "How could Americans be crazy enough to buy such junk?"

I think a more intelligent question would be to wonder how conscious beings like us who will inevitably die could *not* be interested in learning everything we could about what might or might not happen after death, and what that implies for how we live our lives? Yes, of course it's unpleasant to think about death, but trying to ignore the issue and smother our concerns under a surface layer of cynicism, masquerading as scientific or media "objectivity," is not a very healthy psychological strategy. Hopes and fears that fester under the mind's surface become more powerful and pathological in their effects on our lives, not less.

So what kinds of knowledge do we have about death? We have the physical knowledge of the body's death, of course, in more exacting detail than any previous generation, but what happens to our inner self, to our minds, our souls? Here we have two broad classes of knowledge, one we might call (a) opinions and speculations, on the one hand, and (b) scattered bits of *experiential* knowledge on the other. I will include almost all our religious teachings about what happens after death in the opinion and speculation category because the way we learned them, and the way our teachers themselves learned them, is almost entirely a matter of passing on previous ideas with little or no basis in actual experience. Experiential knowledge comes from direct human experience, such as cases of people who have had near death experiences (NDEs). While experiential knowledge tends to eventually get tangled up with and confused with our ideas and theories, we sensibly tend to give it a lot more weight than abstract knowledge. If my car needs repair, I am much more comfortable entrusting it to someone who's had years of experience repairing cars than to someone who's just read about cars extensively or only heard a lot of lectures and opinions about how cars *ought* to function.

So after all the lecturing and theorizing about death is done, what sorts of direct experiences do people have that can give us some understanding of what might happen after death?

NDEs are probably the most direct kind of experiential knowledge about the after death state we can have: they are certainly the most emotionally and intellectually powerful kinds of knowledge that, in some form, we survive death, *for those who experience them.* That's the catch. If you've only read about NDEs or even spoken with some people who've had them, NDEs are very impressive but are back in that first category of opinions and speculations as far as we non-experiencers are concerned, and so don't really still doubts and fears the way direct experiential knowledge does. Logically, it would be quite helpful if we each personally had an NDE, but after an extensive study of NDEs, I don't recommend that. The *near* part of the NDE is too tricky! Most people who come that near to death do not give us an interesting report of what happened afterwards; they get buried!

One aspect of NDEs, the out-of-the-body experience (OBE), is much safer, though, and also carries a lot of conviction about survival of death to those who have it. I have studied hundreds of OBEs in ordinary people over the last thirty years, and one of the most common aftereffects of having an OBE is expressed in statements like this. "I do not *believe* that I will survive death: I *know* I will." The OB experiencer no longer bases her or his expectations about the after death state on opinions and speculations, on beliefs, but rather on her or his own *direct*, personal experience. Most of them do not believe they were physically dead, but they did have the direct experience of temporarily finding themselves located outside their physical bodies and nevertheless having a clear mind, a conscious existence without their physical bodies. To say that this is an impressive experience is to put it mildly! We non-experiencers can take issue with their interpretations of their experiences, but the OB experiencers are not impressed by our doubts: they were there; we are ignorant.

We can learn a lot by studying the reports of those who've had NDEs and OBEs: It's not direct experiential knowledge for us, but at least it's only one step removed from such experiential knowledge. This is a lot more solid than the usual opinions and speculations, even those that bill themselves as scientific theories, where the current opinion is based on a previous person's belief which in turn was based on a previous person's speculations which were wrongly presented as fact or perhaps doctrine, etc., etc., back to antiquity. In most religious beliefs, for example, current doctrine may have been based on someone's actual *experiences* many generations ago, but the accumulations of opinion, interpretation, distortion, and theological editing (probably thought of by the editors as "purification") for compliance with the faith's orthodox doctrines may give us ideas far removed from what actually happened to a real human being once upon a time.

As I mentioned earlier, there is sometimes a problem with studying the reports of those who've had OBEs or NDEs because, like all of us, they tend to get the memories of their direct, experiential knowledge mixed up with their previous and subsequent beliefs *about* their OBEs and NDEs, i.e., they get their facts mixed up with their theories. Sometimes this is obvious. There are writers who are clearly preaching at us and we suspect that, in their righteousness, they have too little respect for what actually happened to them as compared to the beliefs they want to force on us. At the other extreme, some writers clearly take great care to "tell it like it was," to carefully give us as clear and accurate a recounting of the actual experience as possible, and to separate out their ideas and opinions about what it could mean. My friend and colleague Robert A. Monroe, now deceased, was one such person. His classic *Journeys Out of the Body* book is an excellent example of an intelligent, honest and competent person doing his best to make sense out of repeated OBEs. Monroe and a few (they are far too rare, given what we need to know) other pioneers of careful OBE reporting[1] are now joined with this book by Bob Peterson, and our knowledge is thus further enriched. I haven't had the pleasure of meeting Bob Peterson in the flesh yet, but I feel I know him in important ways through reading this book, and I'm quite impressed. Peterson had an apparent NDE as a child which, under the influence of a scientific culture was pushed into the background—but never quite far enough to really destroy his curiosity. Sadly, curiosity about things of the spirit is crushed in too many people today. When he came across information (Monroe's book) about OBEs as an adult, rather than writing off the whole idea as crazy or weird, he decided to try to have the experience, to, in scientific (and *real* common sense) terms, actually become able to look at the facts instead of being satisfied with opinions and speculations. His knowledge of the soul is now much deeper than it was before his OBEs, and, a very important point, he is still puzzled by many aspects of his experiences: Personally, I am more inclined to trust those who admit to puzzlement in life than those who claim to know it all!

A few individuals may have a natural talent for OBEs so it comes easy to them if they try, or is even forced on them. Most of us with an interest might try to have OBEs once or twice, but make no progress and so give up. Peterson worked at it systematically and eventually had hundreds of experiences. This is a reason why this book tells

---

[1] Thorough and clear experiential accounts of repeated OBEs are given in books by Oliver Fox (nom de plume of Hugh Callaway), Joe McMoneagle, Robert A. Monroe and Sylvan Muldoon. Full references to these classics are listed in the bibliography.

us more about the mind and soul than the study of collections of once-in-a-lifetime experiences: Any one OBE is influenced by unknown conditions and beliefs in ways we seldom recognize, but someone with repeated experience can start to separate out what is essential about the OBE and what accidental.

I mentioned earlier that I do not recommend trying to have an NDE because the "near" part is too tricky. But OBEs are much safer, as Peterson reports, and for those of us who are really curious to directly examine the facts, to have an OBE ourselves, Peterson has many exercises in this book that we can try. His honesty shows here too, for he recognizes that these are exercises to try, not guarantees, and that what works for one person may not be helpful for another. But he gives us a wide variety of exercises and is convinced that if we really try them thoroughly, one or more will probably work.

I say that "OBEs are much safer" than NDEs, but they are not, of course, *safe* in any absolute sense. These kinds of direct experiences of things which go beyond everyday reality are both exciting and unsettling, for we do love the habit, routine, and apparent "safety" of the everyday world. If you are reasonably "normal," OBEs will have their frightening moments but probably lead to real growth and spiritual and psychic openings. If you are having difficulty functioning in the everyday world through internal problems, those kind of psychological problems should be solved before trying to venture out of body. The exotic, like OBEs, can be dangerous if we try to use it to bypass ordinary developmental tasks instead of facing them.

But if we seriously try the kinds of OBE inducing exercises Peterson presents and have results? Then "soul"

Out of Body Experiences

will not be just an opinion or speculation for us: Its reality and its implications for living will be experiential *data*. Need I say that the effects on how we live our lives will be rather important?

CHARLES T. TART, PH.D.

Professor Emeritus of Psychology, University of California at Davis

and

Professor, Core Faculty, Institute of Transpersonal Psychology,
Palo Alto, California

FEBRUARY 1997

Introduction to the New Edition

This book is about out-of-body experiences, or OBEs for short. It's also called astral projection in much of the literature. It is not based on folklore or occult tradition, but personal experience. Simply put, an OBE is an experience in which you seem to be consciously apart from your physical body.

People have reported OBEs as part of near death experiences, but other things can trigger them as well. This book will teach you how to induce your own OBEs and what you'll experience once you get there, such as:

- Having a ghostly "astral" body.

- Floating or flying.

- Passing through walls and other solid objects.

- Seeing your own physical body like any other inanimate object in the room.

It's been more than fifteen years since *Out-of-Body Experiences* was first published, but the book is still as relevant today as it was then. The skeptics are still blindly skeptical. The believers still blindly believe. As for scientists, little research has been done. Despite claims from people like Olaf Blanke and Michael Persinger, I still have not seen studies or heard an argument as convincing as the experience itself. I've never asked anyone to believe; experience trumps belief. So try it yourself.

This is where many people ask, "Assuming what you say is true, what good are they? Isn't it all just a waste of time?" The practical applications are unlimited. We can use OBEs to solve crimes, find missing children, and even to fight terrorism. They may even help us unravel the scientific laws of quantum entanglement that psychic abilities only hint at.

Then there's scientific exploration. Consider this: On August 6, 2012, NASA spent two billion dollars to land the rover *Curiosity* on the surface of Mars to learn about that strange foreign world, but it tells us little about our own world, where we're going, or who we are. OBEs tell us more about those things than any interplanetary mission ever can, and while they may not be easy, they're free.

In fact, OBEs are even more relevant than you may realize: while it's doubtful you will ever physically visit Mars, I guarantee you *will* visit a world just as foreign: the afterlife. Most people seem content to rely upon religious dogma—most of which is thousands of years out of date and based on someone else's OBEs—to guide them beyond death. My hope is that someday we will use OBEs to separate religious fact from fiction and replace faith with knowledge so people can stop fighting over religious differences.

There's also a personal side: OBEs have a profound positive impact. People come away with a new attitude toward life, death, and spirituality. I don't value material *things* as much as I do people, experiences, and life-lessons. OBEs do not automatically make you spiritual, but they sure help. All it took was one good look at my own inanimate body to realize we are spiritual beings and the "next life" is not so far off!

Early European sailors believed the Earth was flat. Fearing the unknown, they thought it was dangerous to sail too far west, lest they fall off the edge. After they conquered their fear and went bravely ahead, not only did they discover a whole new world, they also made the transition from two-dimensional thinking to three-dimensional thinking about their reality. Likewise, if we can conquer our fears about OBEs, we will also discover a whole new world, and make the transition from three-dimensional thinking to four-or-more-dimensional thinking about our reality.

This book has two parts. Part 1 is the story of how I changed from skeptic to believer and what I discovered along the way. Part 2 is informational: what other books never told me and what I learned the hard way, such as how seeing and the mind work in an OBE. At the end of each chapter you'll find a simple exercise with tips and techniques. There is also a chapter detailing my most successful OBE technique. Combined, these will help you induce your own OBEs.

OBEs are only limited by how much time and effort you're willing to spend. In thirty-three years, they have never lost their thrill. The adventure goes on. And now, dear readers, it's time to take the out-of-body experience out of the closet!

ROBERT PETERSON
NOVEMBER 2012

Acknowledgments

I'd like to thank the following people for their support:

Kathy Peterson, my wife. Without her support this book would not have been possible.

Robert Monroe, whose books changed my life forever. Even though he's left his body for the last time, his love and dedication are still spreading spirituality throughout this plane.

My brother Joe and his wife Candy for their love and support.

My friends in Phoenix: John, Peggy, Dawn, Patricia, Sabrina, Bob, Cheri, Brad, Bob, Georgann, Jon, Herb, Mary, Judy, Perry, Carol, Jean and everyone else.

LD, wherever you are.

Those who have inspired me with their music: Jon Anderson, Kerry Livgren, Tom Scholz, and Dan Fogelberg.

Part I

From Skeptic to Believer

1

Background

I was born in Minneapolis, Minnesota, and spent the first twenty-four years of my life there. My childhood was normal except for a few unusual experiences that will be described later.

Before I started kindergarten, I met a boy named Brian, who was about three years older, and we became friends. Brian was a good friend, but he had a bad habit of lying. Brian felt that lying made him seem more knowledgeable and important than other kids, and he loved to be in that position of power. At that young age, I was naive and always asking questions, but I had no concept of dishonesty. Hanging around Brian, it didn't take me long to find out what a lie was. Before long, I didn't trust anything that Brian said to me. Still, Brian was my only friend and there were no other kids my age in the area. Instead of abandoning our friendship, I took it as a challenge. I still valued his friendship, but I had to learn to separate fact from fiction. I was forced to use logic to tell when he was lying and when he was telling the truth. Sometimes it worked, and sometimes it didn't. But I got better at it by verifying some of the facts with grownups I knew I could trust.

Before too long, my parents intervened and told me I couldn't see Brian again because he was a "bad influence." They were right. But Brian's friendship taught me some valuable lessons when I was at an impressionable age. First, I learned that you can't believe everything you hear or read. I gained a real appreciation for the "truth," and I learned to question everything. Second, I learned how to use reason, deduction, and logic. My love of the truth turned into a love for scientific knowledge, an insatiable curiosity, and a thirst for knowledge and exploration.

When I entered grade school, I made my first important discovery: the school library. Most of the kids would run to the fiction section to grab the storybooks. I would run to the shelf marked "science" and I'd read textbooks. I would read any book as long as it was scientific: books on dinosaurs, biology, lasers, botany, archeology, astronomy, and anything else that crossed my curious mind in a particular week. Even before I could read, I would learn by looking at the pictures.

My mom used to take me to the public library and let me wander around while she picked out books. Of course, I'd go straight for the science books there too. But in the public library, children's books were mostly storybooks. So I would wander around the adult section and look for science books. I remember one day when I stumbled into the anatomy section of the adult books. I wonder what my parents would have said if they found out I knew all about sex and the reproductive system at the age of six! I remember arguing with other six-year-olds about where babies came from. They insisted on storks and cabbage patches, and I just couldn't talk any sense into them.

I got a reputation for being a "know-it-all" or a "brain." I didn't care for that status at all because people couldn't relate to a "brain" and everyone resents a "know-it-all." I did my best to fight against my reputation and stuck to a small group of friends.

In high school I became interested in the field of computers and my curiosity led me to study computers in my spare time. After taking every short-course the University of Minnesota had to offer, I spent my free time reading computer manuals and writing computer games. My face became well known in the university computer labs. I often chuckled when people twice my age would ask me for help on their programming class assignments.

After high school, I entered the University of Minnesota, majoring in the field of Computer Science. During that time I started having out-of-body experiences (OBEs), and it changed the course of my life. Perhaps it can change your life too!

EXERCISE 1
Affirmations

This "exercise" section, which appears at the end of each chapter, is designed to present exercises and pointers to readers who are interested in learning to have out-of-body experiences. The exercises will be simple in the early chapters and get more complicated in later chapters.

This particular exercise is an affirmation. An affirmation is like a New Year's resolution: something you say to yourself to strengthen your ability to do something. It's not enough just to say the affirmation; you should think about it first, then say it slowly to yourself a few times. Each time you say an affirmation, you should try to put emotion behind your words and actually believe what you are saying.

Using affirmations works for many reasons. First, it's a way to clearly communicate with your subconscious, and we all know how powerful the subconscious is from hypnosis studies.[2]

Second, many people in metaphysics believe in a higher consciousness, sometimes called your "Higher Self," or "Oversoul," which is even more powerful than your subconscious. Affirmations also allow you to communicate your intentions to your oversoul which can help you reach your goals. I also believe that your oversoul has its own goals that are tied to

---

[2] For useful material on hypnosis, see *Altered States of Consciousness*, edited by Charles Tart.

your spiritual growth, and that it is more likely to help you if you agree to help it accomplish its goals.

Third, many people in metaphysics believe that your beliefs directly affect your experience. Affirmations make it easier to change your belief system and make positive changes in your life.

Because affirmations are such a powerful influence on your subconscious mind, you should carefully avoid sending yourself negative messages. One of the first affirmations I ever used was, "I am very loose from my body." The message seemed innocent enough, but I discovered I had an underlying negative belief that being loose from my body meant that I was not quite healthy. After a few days of using this affirmation, I started feeling disoriented, dizzy, and on the verge of becoming sick. Luckily, I figured out what was happening and changed my affirmation!

The most effective affirmations are the kind you make for yourself. They should be short, succinct, and stated in a positive way. State the changes you want in your life, as if they are already yours. For example, use "I can" messages instead of "I don't want" messages. Also, affirm what you are willing to do to make it real. For this exercise, do affirmations based on your desire to have OBEs. You can either create your own affirmation or use the one given below.

> I can easily leave my body. Out-of-body experiences come naturally to me. To prepare, I will practice OBE exercises, cooperate with the universe, follow my impulses, act on my intuitions, share my knowledge, spread my love, and cooperate with my own Higher Self.

2

My Childhood

I grew up in a hectic house with three brothers and one sister. My dad was a religious man in his own quiet way. He generally kept quiet about his religion. Once or twice I heard him mention Edgar Cayce in passing, but I ignored most of this, dismissing it as either "occult" or "unscientific." As a rule, he never exposed his kids to occult ideas.

My mom was a devout Catholic, and she raised her kids as "good" Catholics, that is, the kind who go to church every Sunday, say their prayers, and pretty much forget about God and religion during the week. At any rate, I grew up with a healthy sense of right and wrong, and never used drugs. I was the only kid in my high school who never tried marijuana. I still haven't tried drugs; drugs are for people who are uninformed about OBEs or lack the will to induce their own, natural altered states of consciousness.

Once I asked my mom if she remembered anything unusual about my childhood. She told me that whenever I got really sick, I would sleepwalk. To be precise, I would get up in the middle of the night and dance around in circles chanting like an Indian shaman. Of course, I wasn't conscious at the time.

I only remember that when I got sick, a strange sensation used to terrify me: when I drifted off to sleep, I had a terrifying "nightmare." I would "dream" that I held a tiny grain of salt in the palm of my hand. Then my consciousness would shrink to an incredibly small size until the grain of salt looked like a skyscraper. Terrified of being crushed by the salt, I would wake up screaming.

I didn't consider myself a psychic child. Nonetheless, I had a few experiences worth noting.

One day, when I was perhaps ten or twelve years old, I was very depressed. I don't even remember why, but my depression was so severe that I actually prayed to die. Sometime after I had gone to bed, I awoke to find myself whooshing up, out of my body, escorted by what I thought was an angel. I thought I had died, and I was amazed that I hadn't felt any pain during the separation. I thought that death would be painful, but it wasn't.

Finally I came to a halt before a large, tremendously powerful, invisible being, who I immediately thought was God. The being told me it was time to go, and I understood immediately what that meant: death.

Then I got a yearning to go back. I was homesick. I felt guilty about wishing to die. And I knew that my parents would be very sad about my death. So I begged and pleaded to be brought back to earth. "Why?" I was asked. I thought for a moment, searching for an answer. I said, "Everyone there thinks that death is painful and sad. I have to go back to tell everyone that death is painless and joyful."

After thinking about it, "God" consented and I was escorted back. I awoke amazed at the realism of my experience. I forced myself to believe it was a dream and nothing more.

Out of Body Experiences

Another experience happened when I was a little older, perhaps fourteen or fifteen. I used to have playful wrestling matches with two other boys. One day we were talking about wrestling and got on the subject of the world-famous wrestling hold called "the sleeper hold." The hold would knock an opponent out by cutting off blood circulation to the brain. Anyway, we all wondered what it would be like to be knocked out. FD was the strongest of the three and the third boy was afraid, so I agreed to let FD knock me out with a bear-hug.

We went outside and he gave me the strongest bear-hug I've ever experienced. I couldn't breathe and soon became unconscious. It was like waking from a dream; this world was a dream and I awoke to a reality more real and vivid than this world was. I saw the illusion of this existence on earth dispelled! It faded away and I didn't regret it. Soon I found myself in the "real" world in a huge city that I already knew.

My memory seemed to return—yes, I had gone to sleep and dreamed of a little place called "earth" and now I was awake. "That was a silly dream," I thought, and I soon forgot all about "earth." I continued my life, just like it was before I fell asleep. I lived in that fantastic city for years and years—centuries it seemed. I lived there so long that I *completely* forgot about earth. For hundreds of years I had forgotten earth. If someone asked me about it, I couldn't remember, since I had left it so long ago.

Then one day I was walking to a store. Suddenly I became confused, losing my sense of direction, and I felt myself falling. Abruptly I opened my eyes only to see strange leaves, the sky, and FD and the other boy looking at me! Where was I now? How did I get here? What happened? Then I remembered: hundreds of years ago, I fell asleep and found myself here. This place was called "earth" and was a part of a weird dream. I must have fallen asleep again. Slowly my earthly memory returned. I asked the boys how long I had been unconscious. They said only a few minutes. They asked me what happened, and I told them I didn't want to talk about it.

A third psychic experience was as follows: I was riding with my father in his truck, and we went under a railroad bridge viaduct in Columbia Heights, Minnesota, only a few blocks from where I lived in Minneapolis. As we drove under the bridge, a train was passing over the track. I got a very uncomfortable feeling and "imagined" the train falling from the track onto the truck and street, crushing us. "I hate this," I said to my dad. After we had gone through the viaduct I asked him, "How often do they jump the track?" My dad (who worked as a clerk for a railroad) said that it was nearly impossible for a train to derail; it was especially rare at a bridge or viaduct. Within a week, a train derailed at that very viaduct. I was about fourteen at the time.

Some people may say that these psychic experiences would suggest I was born with some natural abilities. However, I disagree. A couple of unusual events during childhood does not make you "psychic." My childhood was normal.

Once when I was young, I overheard my dad talking to my brother, and he mentioned something called "astral projection." I asked my brother what it was, but he brushed me aside with a simple, "That's where people fly outside their bodies." It sounded interesting to me, but too unscientific—like a fairy tale. I waited patiently until the next time my mom took me to the library, then I tried to find "astral" in the card catalog. The library didn't have any books on it at the time, so I forgot all about it.

EXERCISE 2
Prayer

Many people from all walks of life believe that we have spiritual guides or guardians of some sort. Christians call them guardian angels. Zoroastrians call them the Fervashi. Spiritualists call them spirit guides. Whatever we call them, they can hear our silent thoughts and prayers, and they can help us in many ways. They can even help us have OBEs.

Since our guides are here to help us spiritually, this exercise is to pray to your guides to help you have OBEs. I can't tell you what to pray, but I can give you an example that I sometimes use:

> I pray to God, the All That Is, and to my guides, helpers, and any other benevolent beings, to please help me achieve my goal of exploring consciously while out of my body. Help me to leave my body and become conscious, and in return, I will do my best to become more spiritual and help you with your goals of guidance.

3

First Contact

It wasn't until September 9, 1979 that the subject of out-of-body experiences came up again. My brother Joe knew my dad was interested in the occult, so for Father's Day, Joe gave him the book, *Journeys Out of the Body*, by Robert A. Monroe. I remembered searching the card catalog for books on this topic as a child, so after my dad had finished reading it, I asked him if I could borrow it, and he said yes.

Monroe explained his OBEs in such a logical, scientific manner that I read the book faster than I'd ever read before. I didn't really believe Monroe's claims, but I liked his approach. His book urged me not to take his word for it, but to try it myself.

I decided to take Monroe up on his offer, and follow his techniques to see for myself if these experiences were real or just hype, fantasy, or dreams. That night, before I went to bed, I attempted astral projection for the first time. I had memorized Monroe's method earlier, and I decided to close my eyes and try it.

The first step was to relax. I spent a long time relaxing completely. The next step, which was quite a bit harder, was to drift between waking and sleeping consciousness.

I found myself drifting into sleep once or twice, and I yanked myself back to full consciousness each time, being careful not to move my fully relaxed body. It took quite awhile before I felt comfortable enough to go on to the next step: clearing my mind of all thoughts.

This was harder yet. Every time I heard a noise I would be distracted, and my mind would start to wander. Then my body started itching in the most distracting way. As soon as I'd scratch an itch, another new itch would take its place. Even after I conquered most of my itches (and ignored the rest), it was hard to keep my mind from wandering.

At one point, I found I could hold my mind blank for several minutes, and I decided that would be long enough to go on to the next step: using imaginary lines of force to call "the vibrations." I followed Monroe's method to the letter, carefully pausing between each step in the process. I was just about to give up when I felt a heavy "*twang*" in my head. It felt as if the lines of force had somehow become real and had touched a 110-volt power line. I thought, "Oops. Maybe this isn't such a good idea." I tried to pull myself back to normal consciousness by retracting my imaginary lines of force.

I quickly pulled the lines of force back toward me, but much to my surprise, the "electricity" I felt at the end of those lines was also being pulled toward me. It was as if I were fishing and felt a sharp bite at the end of my fishing pole: I quickly tried to pull my fishing line out of the water, but I only managed to set the hook and pull in a fish. And it was quite a fish: a kind of electrical "vibration" violently swept into my body, filling it with an electric-like shock and a terrible roaring noise. I thought I was being electrocuted and my first reaction was sheer panic. I could hear my heart beating wildly in mad fear, but I was powerless to control it.

Somehow I could see through my closed eyelids. I looked up and saw a blue ring of electrical fire flying right toward my head. It was about a foot in diameter, with the energy sparks about an inch-and-a-half thick, and it was bright blue. I instinctively tried to raise my arms to protect myself from the impact, but I found myself paralyzed and unable to move my arms. The ring of blue energy started to slip over my forehead and I looked away, afraid to see what would happen next. I started fighting wildly to regain control of my body, and the "vibrations" slowly smoothed down and died out. When the vibrations faded completely, I could move my body again.

I shook my arms and legs, and rejoiced that I hadn't lost the ability to move them, happy that I was completely in my body. "My God," I thought to myself, "It worked! Monroe wasn't lying! There *are* other worlds!"

EXERCISE 3
Relaxation

A key factor in leaving the body is relaxation. The body needs to be relaxed as completely as possible. If the physical body isn't completely relaxed, it may be very difficult to turn your focus away from the body.

Some laboratory experiments suggest that the physical body may be even more relaxed during an OBE than it is during a normal sleep state.[3] Learning to relax your body to such a degree (without falling asleep) can be difficult, but it has its rewards. Learning to physically relax can lower blood pressure and counteract stress. You'll feel better and live longer by practicing relaxation regularly.

For this exercise, you should learn to relax your body at will, completely and quickly. Learn to relax every fiber and tissue of your body. One common method of relaxation is to get into a comfortable position and slowly go through every limb from the feet up, tensing and relaxing every muscle in that limb.

Take special care to completely relax the muscles in your face, including your eyelids, forehead, and jaw muscles. It's all right to open your mouth for maximum relaxation.

---

[3] For instance, in some OBE experiments done by Charles Tart, subjects reportedly had lower skin resistance during OBEs than during sleep. Skin resistance is a reasonable measurement of relaxation in the body. It is measured with BSR (basal skin resistance) or GSR (galvanic skin resistance) devices. Another use for these relaxation testing devices is in Polygraph ("lie detector") tests. See "A Psychological Study of Out-of-the-Body Experiences in a Selected Subject," by Charles Tart, in the *Journal of the American Society for Psychical Research*, Vol. 62, No. 1, 1968.

After finishing this first relaxation, go back and slowly check every muscle again, making sure it's relaxed. If there is tension in any muscle, repeat the procedure and check every muscle again.

4

Beliefs Blown to Bits

After my experience with the vibrations, I got up out of bed and walked into the living room to tell somebody, anybody, that it was all real. My mom was already in bed sleeping; and my dad was asleep in his favorite chair in front of the television, and I didn't want to wake him. I walked into the kitchen and got a glass of water, occasionally shaking my arms and legs to make sure I was completely inside my body. After a few minutes I walked back to my bedroom and lay down, but I could not sleep. I could not stop thinking about the encounter and its implications.

First, it was the most terrifying experience of my life. It felt like the vibrations were harming my body, and the roaring, hissing sound only scared me more. I had confronted humankind's two biggest fears: fear of the unknown and fear of death. My scientific self couldn't make any scientific sense out of the experience—it was not part of the physical universe that I knew. I tried to think about it based on my Catholic beliefs that insisted I could only leave my body if I died. Did I just have a close encounter with death? After several hours of trying to make sense out of the experience, I fell asleep with no answers.

I spent the next day arguing with myself about the experience. My whole belief system was blown to pieces. Seeing is believing, and I could not deny that I had experienced the vibrations, the hissing sound, the paralysis, and the blue ring of energy. I even "saw" through my closed eyelids. I knew I was not hallucinating, I was not insane, I was not dreaming, and I was not under hypnosis. My experience was very "real" to me, as real as my normal waking consciousness, if not more so.

My first observation was that some kind of nonphysical reality existed. That observation was a direct contradiction of my scientific beliefs because science had been leading me to believe there was no such thing as a nonphysical reality.

Furthermore, I reasoned, Einstein's theory of relativity says that matter is the same as energy. If a person could consciously leave his body and enter a truly nonphysical world, he wouldn't exactly be "matter" or "energy" as we know it. Science left no room for "consciousness" or "spirit" in its formulas. Science led me to believe that there were only three basic dimensions of experience (plus time) and five senses. Everything else was labeled superstition, nonsense, hallucination, or possibly religion.

There is a fact of logic that when a premise is wrong, any conclusions made from that premise are also wrong. Since I had discovered a premise of science that was incorrect, or at the very best incomplete, I deduced that many or all of the conclusions made by modern science were also wrong. At the very least, they were ignoring some major facts.

My own scientific training had led me to distrust science itself! I could no longer trust the textbooks I loved as a child! Nevertheless, I believe that if a system works, it is okay to use it until you find something that works better. I decided that I would still use the scientific method as a tool but never completely trust science again. Meanwhile, the only thing I could do to find peace of mind was to try to induce more out-of-body experiences and learn more about the nonphysical world.

My inner turmoil didn't end with my scientific belief system. I was Catholic. And that caused its own complications.

The Catholic system taught me to believe in one "heaven," one "hell," and one earth. On judgment day, they said, God judges a person to be either "good" or "bad." The people labeled "bad" go to hell forever, and the people labeled "good" go to heaven forever. And of course, until you die, you spend your days on earth.

I could guess what the Catholics would say about a nonphysical reality. The liberal Catholics would probably say that I was being absurd, and they had science to back them up. Fundamentalists would probably say that any such experience must surely be the work of the Devil, trying to lead my soul into sin.

Still, I refused to believe I was being tricked: seeing is believing. I had seen that a nonphysical place existed and it wasn't "heaven" or "hell." Therefore, I had also found a basic premise of Catholicism that was wrong. I decided not to trust what the Catholics had taught me because they were just as ignorant of this nonphysical world as I had been.

I continued going to church for a while, but I started an intense examination of my Catholic beliefs. Hoping to find some answers, I found a Bible that I got as a confirmation gift, and I read the entire New Testament and much of the Old Testament. The Bible convinced me that Jesus was a good man who taught good lessons. In fact, I agreed with everything that Jesus was supposed to have said.

But even what I read in the Bible didn't agree with my Catholic belief system! Heavy questions nagged in my heart. Why does the Catholic church insist that Jesus is the Son of God, when Jesus called himself the "son of man" repeatedly? Why do they pray, "Lord, I am not worthy to receive you," then immediately they receive Him? Why do they pray for their own petty interests instead of entrusting that God would take care of the world? Why do they preach about needing to *fear* God? Why do they hold carnivals and bingo games when Jesus said not to use a place of worship in these ways and even kicked money changers out of a temple? Why, indeed, do they pass a money plate in church? Why do they spend millions and millions of dollars on grandiose churches—have you ever seen St. Peter's Basilica?—when people are starving? Why do they call the pope "our holy father" when Jesus said not to call anyone father (Matthew 23:9)?

Why do the Catholics go to church and pray in public when Jesus said, "when you pray, go into a room by yourself . . . in your secret place" (Matthew 6:5). Why do people go to church on Sunday and act unspiritual the rest of the week? It seemed wrong that, as a Catholic, going to church was my obligation and, once this obligation was fulfilled, I was free to be as mundane and unspiritual as I wanted. Just one out-of-body experience blasted that whole hypocritical concept out of the water. During my OBE, I saw that I *was* a spiritual being—in fact, I was a spirit—and the thought of dying without some *real* relationship with God was scary. Before my OBE, it was enough to recite prayers I didn't even understand. After my OBE, it was clear I needed to do more.

Eventually I came to realize that my Catholic belief system was not spiritual at all. The closer I looked, the more I understood. So I stopped going to church and embarked on a truly spiritual path. I don't mean to imply that all Catholics are unspiritual. It's just that I needed to find my own answers.

Since my OBE caused me to have a real concern with spiritual matters, I realized that it had taught me to be more spiritual, not less. I decided that God would not send me to hell for leaving the church and finding my own spiritual path.

I resolved to ignore the pain, ignore the fear, ignore the danger, and take my chances with death and damnation to discover the truth. I decided to keep trying every night until I got more results. Meanwhile, I decided to "raid" the Minneapolis Public Library to find more information on OBEs and other methods of producing them.

EXERCISE 4
Pretend Day

If you've read any other books on astral projection, you may have wondered: why have almost all OBE techniques been an exercise of the imagination? Why are there so many visualizations? Why is pretending so important to leaving the body?

Well, first let me make myself perfectly clear: OBEs are a lot more than just pretend; they are real. Absolutely real. If you've had one, there will be no doubt in your mind. During the OBE, you are as wide-awake, alert, and conscious as you are while reading this. Sometimes more so. All this pretending is just a stepping-stone to get you out of your body.

Before talking about pretending, I'd like to expose another myth. Some occult books say that children can leave their bodies easily but it's harder for most adults. They therefore conclude that as you get older, you become more cemented in your physical body. They say the older you get, the harder it is to have OBEs because we become more focused in our body. Well, that just isn't true. People who say that are using an excuse to be lazy and not practice.

Why, then, don't adults have more OBEs? One reason is that adults don't use their imagination as much or as vividly as children. That doesn't mean we can't use our imaginations well; it just means that most people don't.

There's something magical about the imagination. Children know that intuitively. It's a matter of focus. Children use their imagination to unfocus from their daily lives. They know how to daydream and pretend. That's why children are so psychic! And we can become that psychic—that aware—if we start exercising our playful imaginations too.

This exercise isn't just for now, it's an all-day exercise. I want you to make today "Pretend Day." All day today, at every available opportunity, I want you to exercise your playful imagination. These little pretend skits don't have to be long. It's better to be short and frequent, than long and drawn out. I'll give you some examples. Go through your day doing these sorts of things:

The next time you sit down, just pretend for a few short seconds that you fall through your chair (in your astral body) and find yourself on the ground or through the floor. The next time you open a door, playfully pretend that your hand passes through the door knob instead of grabbing it. The next time you walk up a flight of stairs, playfully pretend you glide up it smoothly without walking. Pretend that your astral body glides up the stairs and patiently waits for your physical body to arrive at the top. The next time you look in a mirror, pretend you are looking at your physical body from afar. Pretend you are astral in as many instances as you can.

Also, it's good to pretend non-OBE things today. For instance, the next time you take a drive in your car, pretend that it lifts off the ground and starts flying over the traffic. The next time you are stopped by a traffic light, pretend that you get out a gun and shoot it!

Use your playful imagination at every available opportunity today, and where possible, work in out-of-body themes such as flying, floating, or passing through physical matter.

5

Pokes and Prods

M onroe said that fear is the biggest barrier to the out-of-body experience, and I soon found out why. If I were somehow able to leave my body, and Monroe can leave his, how many more people are "out there," and what can they do to me while I am out there? It also made sense that when a person's body dies, they are forced to have a permanent OBE. What could these spirits do to me? Furthermore, what could happen to my body while I am out? Could somebody else get inside my body while I am out? These were some questions that crossed my mind during the two months after my first encounter.

During those two months I had my first dream about having an OBE. I dreamed I was dreaming. In the second-level dream, I was telling my brother how I often attempted OBEs, and I showed him how to concentrate. Then I felt my chest rise. I thought of it rising more and it did. My dream-self then came out of my body, which was in the bed of the first-level dream. I started walking toward my door, when I was pulled back inside my body by the cord. I thought, "Good. Now I can wake up and record that I've been out of my body." However, when I woke up I knew it was only a dream. It paled in comparison to my first episode with the vibrations. Still, having a dream about an OBE was fun, and I knew that later I could compare it to a real OBE. Little did I know that my first real OBE was just around the corner.

Although I didn't have another out-of-body experience during those two months, I did run into some unexpected and frightening sensations and experiences. These sensations weren't bad—just startling. They often jarred me out of the near-OBE state and spoiled the whole OBE attempt. Sometimes it felt as if a warm hand was being placed on my body. I even felt a few pinches on my butt!

One night I followed Monroe's procedure to the letter and was making good progress toward leaving my body. Suddenly I became very aware and alert. My eyes were closed and I was moving deeper into the blackness that I saw ahead of me, into a deeper state of consciousness. Suddenly, I heard an authoritative voice say, "STOP!" How could I argue? I never expected to be hearing voices during these experiments. I panicked and did everything I could to force myself back to a normal state.

Another night I was trying to blank my mind without much success. After a while, I started to feel a swaying sensation, as if some part of my consciousness was rocking gently. I tried to increase the swaying, but the more I tried, the less I swayed. When I quit trying, the swaying would get stronger again. The swaying sensation was very much like the "sea-legs" sensation that sailors experience when they've been on a ship too long and try to sleep on shore. After some experimentation I managed to change the direction of the swaying from side to side instead of up and down. The sensation was strange, but I could see no harm in it. From then on, I could start the swaying sensation quite easily once I relaxed enough during practice.

One day, after spending many hours on a boat, I was feeling the "sea-legs" phenomenon and decided to compare it with my new type of swaying. When I got into bed and started my new swaying, I could feel both sensations at the same time. The "sea legs" caused my brain to feel an artificial swaying sensation, but at the same time, my new swaying also caused another separate rocking sensation. In a way, it felt almost as if I had two astral bodies that were swaying at the same time.

Several times I induced a strange bodily vibration that stemmed from my relaxation technique of tensing and relaxing my entire body. I wondered if this vibration was related to the true OBE vibrations. The answer came one night when I decided to conduct an experiment in which I tried to watch myself fall asleep.

I relaxed and just kept going deeper and deeper toward sleep. Suddenly, against my will, I was "zapped" into a state of full awareness. Then I felt a slight tingling. Then the vibrations came without my "reaching" for them. This time I noticed that the "true" vibrations were a crackling, electrical vibration. It felt as if electrical currents were disrupting my body, but not painfully, and not harming it. I tried to strengthen the vibrations with my mind. I managed to get them a little stronger, but like my first encounter, I could hear (but not feel) that my heart was pounding wildly. This broke my train of thought and the vibrations faded, as if my idle thinking (or worrying) drove them off.

One night I got to the point where my mind wouldn't wander. I heard some banging sounds in my room that I couldn't explain. Suddenly I heard a louder, more defined bang that seemed to come from the ground, about five feet from the bed. I directed my senses in that direction and "felt" a big presence there, as if a spirit or ghost of some sort were there. I was afraid, but I tried to control my emotions, and asked in my mind who it was and what its purpose was. There was no answer. I forced myself back to full consciousness and looked in that direction, where I saw a filmy, undefined movement. By then, I was so afraid that I purposely started moving parts of my body to make sure I wouldn't leave my body. I tried my hardest to find a physical, logical explanation for all of this without success. Naturally, it took me a while to calm down and dare to shut my eyes to go to sleep.

At other times, I started noticing strange tugging sensations during OBE practice. It felt as if someone was pulling at my clothes or hair during practice. The sensation seemed to have something to do with the swaying motion. It felt as if something or someone was pulling on whatever was swaying. It was as if my astral body was being tugged while I was still fully in my body.

I also started feeling "pressures" similar to the tugging sensations. When this happened, it seemed as if heavy weights were placed on various parts of my body: my forehead, my feet, my chest. Sometimes if I didn't move, these pressures would become painful after a few minutes.

With practice I became better at producing the vibrations. I noticed that just before the vibrations came, I was always "zapped" into a state of acute alertness. Sometimes it seemed as if my consciousness was focused into an oval disk at my body's face. But every time the vibrations would come, my heart would start pounding, I would panic, and the vibrations would slowly fade until I was back to normal. When I opened my eyes, they were cloudy but slowly cleared up. My body felt very heavy and stiff. My hands were stiff and hard to open. Sometimes I was also slightly dizzy after the experience.

I started noticing another strange sensation while trying to leave my body: a ringing noise in my ears. I quickly learned to reproduce the ringing, but it never got me anywhere, so I learned to ignore it.

Another thing I've experienced during practice is sudden falling sensations. I would be quietly attempting an OBE, and suddenly it would feel as if a trap door had sprung open, and I would panic-fall about three feet. After three feet, I would be startled back to full consciousness with a slight jump, as if my astral body was slapped back into the physical body. This had a simple variation that was more common: sometimes it seemed as if my consciousness was thrown three to five feet forward or backward.

Sometimes I heard very loud rushing or roaring noises in my head. Usually when this happened, I also felt as if my consciousness was being crushed in on all sides. It was as if the very boundaries of my awareness were forced down to a tiny infinitesimal pinpoint in the center of my head.

A friend told me of a few jarring sensations that sometimes disturb her just before OBEs. The first sensation she described as feeling as though her heart was "pulling apart" or expanding. The second sensation is loss of breath, as if the astral body does not breathe and she loses all awareness of bodily breathing. She also says that her whole field of vision sometimes shrinks suddenly, like a camera shutter.

Trying to ignore these sensations is like trying to ignore a slap in the face. I discovered that the best thing to do is to acknowledge them, but remain passive and not let them startle me and ruin the OBE attempt. When I finally learned to get through these sensations calmly, they started leading me to conscious astral projection!

A positive outcome of all the frightening experiences was that they helped me get over my fear. I was forced to face my fears and conquer them one by one, especially my fear of the unknown.

EXERCISE 5
Daily Visualizations

Much of the occult literature concerning out-of-body experiences claims that we leave our bodies every night during sleep, but we usually are not conscious during these nightly excursions. Usually the OBE happens only after our consciousness has been disabled. But sometimes something goes wrong with the process, and a piece of our conscious self retains awareness during the separation. At those times, we often "wake up" abruptly with a jolt before we are fully asleep.

One of the "tricks" to having out-of-body experiences is getting your subconscious mind to wake you up after you are out of your body. Quite simply, if you can influence your subconscious mind to reinstate your conscious awareness once the process of separation is complete, you will have fully conscious OBEs.

There are several approaches to influencing the subconscious mind. In previous exercises, we used affirmations and prayers to influence the subconscious mind (and to influence other things as well). Hypnosis is another excellent approach. Early studies in hypnosis showed a lot of promise in inducing OBEs. Unfortunately, there have been very few experiments in this area to the best of my knowledge, and the literature is scarce.

There are several audio hypnosis tapes available for inducing OBEs.[4] I'm fairly resistant to hypnosis, so I

---

[4] See bibliography for more information on OBE induction tapes.

haven't had any results using these tapes. The closest I've experienced was remote viewing[5] which, I think, isn't nearly as fun as astral projection.

Another way to influence the subconscious is through concentrated visualizations, done frequently throughout the day. Any visualization that is OBE-related is good. Here are a few I use:

1. Visualize yourself flying over valleys, seas, plains.

2. Visualize yourself shooting out away from your body.

3. Visualize yourself floating.

4. Sit down and visualize yourself taking a step back and standing up so that you are looking down at the back of your head. Then think to yourself, "That's not me. That's just a shell."

Practice holding onto visualizations as long as you can. See how "real" you can make the visualization. These skills are very valuable for learning to induce OBEs.

---

[5] Remote viewing, known in the past as "traveling clairvoyance," is a visual type of ESP. The subject actually sees the location he or she is visiting, but remains in full bodily consciousness. For more information on remote viewing, see the book, *Mind Trek*, by Joe McMoneagle.

6

My First Out-of-Body Experience

The morning of November 1, 1979, started out normally. I woke up around 7:00 A.M., followed my usual morning routine and caught a bus to the University of Minnesota. I got to the university at 9:00 A.M., walked into my favorite computer lab, and started programming. I worked furiously on a microcomputer game for several hours until it was time for my Thursday class. I hurried off to class, took copious notes during class, then hurried back to the computer lab.

This time I logged into the university's time-sharing computer and started working on another game I wrote. A hockey game was playing on a radio in the back of the lab. I worked on that computer game until 10:00 P.M. that night. After twelve hours of intense programming, I started getting tired and hungry. I hadn't eaten since breakfast. I signed off the computer and caught the next bus home.

When I got home at 10:30 P.M., I was hungry. I looked in the refrigerator and found a big pan of lasagna. My mom must have made me a big lasagna dinner, and I missed it by staying late at the university! I took out a big slice of lasagna, heated it, and wolfed it down. Ordinarily I would have made my usual attempt to leave my body, but that night I was just too tired. I went to bed at 11:30 P.M. and was asleep the minute my head hit the pillow.

I fell into a deep sleep and started dreaming a programmer's most hated and feared dream—the programming dream. The same dream plagued me for hours: I was sitting at a computer terminal, asking myself, "How can I make this program better?"

I put up with that dream for four annoying hours. That was all I could stand. I became so annoyed by this dream that I couldn't take any more. Slowly I turned my attention away from the dream. I slowly forced myself to become conscious, but as I did, I noticed the dream was still going on! Somehow I was awake and asleep at the same time!

What happened next is hard to describe. My consciousness was split into five parts. Each part was separate and unique, yet I was each of them simultaneously. Each was thinking its own thoughts and communicating with the other four. All five of "me" were arguing about the computer game and how to make it better!

The feeling was beyond words: I was five personalities at the same time, and I was talking to myself! One of my five selves asked, "Well, how can we make the space-war game better?" Another "me" said, "Well, I think we should allow more interactive communication between spaceships." Yet another "me" replied, "No, I think it's more important to improve the fighting ability of the computer-controlled opponent ships." One of my five selves was bored to tears watching this whole conversation and tried to force itself to consciousness. Now that

"I" was conscious, I was fascinated at what was happening: I was conscious and split into five parts, and each part was taking turns talking.

At first I tried to follow the conversation, but something strange started happening. As I became more conscious, my four other selves seemed to speed up![6] I tried to keep up with the conversation, but the talking became faster and faster. Soon the four voices sounded like a tape player in fast-forward mode, and I lost track of what they were saying. Meanwhile, the voices faded into the distance and seemed to disappear.

My consciousness was no longer split. I was completely awake and aware of my surroundings, but I knew something was not normal My body felt unusual. It felt odd to be conscious and yet still asleep.

Just then, I got a strange feeling all over, like a shiver over my whole body. I listened to see if I could hear what caused the strange feeling. I heard what sounded like a hockey announcer in the background! I thought, "Now that's odd. Where could that be coming from?" I wondered if the sound could be coming from the bathroom where we kept a small radio. It sounded a little bit too loud for that; the radio had to be closer to my bedroom.

I wondered if a radio was playing in our dining room, which was next to my bedroom. That didn't make sense because there weren't any radios in that room. Besides, the radio seemed a bit too loud for that, too. I figured the radio must be in my bedroom somewhere.

---

[6] I have a theory about why the dream conversation seemed to speed up. Rapid eye movements (REMs) seem to indicate that some dreams happen to us at high speed, although to us they seem normal speed. They may also indicate that our subconscious thoughts can be much faster than our conscious thoughts. As I became conscious, I started to notice the difference in speeds.

I thought for a moment that my little alarm clock/ radio might have turned on in the night, but it seemed too loud even for that. It was loud enough to be my stereo, but I remembered turning it off before going to bed. Besides, when I listened closer, the hockey announcer sounded even closer than my stereo.

As I listened, the sound of the hockey announcer's voice grew louder and louder as if someone were turning up the volume steadily. I started to worry as the sound became louder and louder, until finally my ears were hurting and I was ready to scream with the pain.

Suddenly it stopped and I experienced complete and total silence. Another strange feeling came over me: I felt like I was completely separate from my body, although I was still occupying the same space. I decided to try to get out.

I had read a few OBE books by then. Some of them had good techniques to separate the consciousness from the body, but none of them said what to do next! How could I get away from the body I was lying in? Since I was in my astral body, gravity didn't affect me, so I didn't just "fall" out of the body. My astral body could pass right through physical matter, so I didn't think I could grab onto anything to pull myself out. I didn't think I could push my way out either; what could I push against?

I thought about the problem for a few minutes. Then I examined my physical body and noticed that it seemed solid on the outside edges. The edges looked like a barrier of gray. My physical body seemed like a bottle; it was solid on the outside, but hollow on the inside. I was like the liquid inside the bottle, fluid and elastic, but there was no way out of the bottle!

At first I tried to twist myself inside the physical body so I could climb out the stomach. I wiggled my astral arms out of the physical arms, like taking off a tight sweater. Then I squirmed until I was under the rib cage. I reached my astral arms up, and tried to claw my way through the stomach. I clawed and clawed, but some barrier, some force-field, was holding me back. The harder I struggled against the barrier, the more impossible it seemed to move. I managed to inch my way for a little while but gave up and lay down again.

I decided to try another way out. I lifted my legs over my head, and did a backward somersault over my head and out of my body.

I felt free and weightless. I wanted to float slowly up to the ceiling. With that thought, I started to float gently up. Then I looked up and thought about my destination, the top of the ceiling. Suddenly, I whooshed up to the ceiling. I looked around the room with a sense of delight.

I looked straight down at my body. It was under the bed covers, but from what I could see, it looked as if it had just collapsed and was out cold. I thought, "Gee, what if I fall from up here?" As soon as the thought crossed my mind, I came crashing down into my physical body and rejoined. I went right into a short, dreamless sleep. In a minute or two I woke up in my physical body. Being a skeptic, I asked myself, "Was that a hallucination? Did I dream it all?" No way. It was real beyond my wildest expectations of real.

I rolled over and looked at the time. It was 3:45 in the morning.

I recalled the whole incident three or four times. During the experience I was perfectly cool, calm, and collected. That is, until I crashed into my body. Now that

I was safely in my body, I felt the full realization of what had happened: I had literally been outside my body. The more I thought about it, the more scary it seemed. My heart was still pounding with excitement. However, I was more tired than I was afraid, so I managed to calm myself down enough to drift back to sleep.

The next thing I knew, the computer conversation dream started again! This time I realized right away what was happening and I was immediately "zapped" out of my physical body again. Like before, I was separate from my body, but still lying inside it. I was too cautious to get up and walk around outside my body, but I didn't want to waste the opportunity to explore. I decided to do some experiments while still lying inside my body.

The first experiment was a simple one: I wanted to see if I could lift my astral arms and look at them. If I could see them, what would they look like?

I bent my astral arms at the elbow and looked at them. They looked and felt perfectly normal and natural. They seemed so normal that after shaking them a few times, I convinced myself I was back inside my body! I thought, "There's nothing unusual about this; I'm perfectly fine. I'm not out of my body—how silly of me." I tried to lower my arms, but I couldn't! It seemed as if my arms were held in some kind of force-field! I pushed and pushed, trying to force my arms down to their normal position, but the harder I tried, the more resistance I felt: I could only move them two inches in a circle at best. Then I really panicked! I drew up as much strength as I could to use it against the force-field. With all the energy I could muster, I forcefully slammed my arms back into place.

I blacked out for a second and went back to full body consciousness. Again I asked myself, "Was it real?" It was so real that I convinced myself I was inside my body! Why did my arms get stuck? I'm not sure. Perhaps I was so sure I was in the physical body that I became part-physical and part-astral, and my arms were held in limbo.

As I thought about the experience over and over, I wondered, "Why don't the OBE books mention anything about this?"

My first two out-of-body experiences were achieved by becoming conscious during a dream. This is known in today's literature as lucid dreaming. This method of leaving the body was documented in the early 1900s in books and articles by Oliver Fox (a pen name for Hugh Calloway) and Yram (a pen name for Marcel Louis Forhan). I didn't read those books until after my first experiences. Up until that point I thought the only way to have an OBE was through conscious effort. I will say more about lucid dreams in chapters 12 and 26.

EXERCISE 6
Imaginary Vibrations

Many people have described the out-of-body exit as a raising of vibrations. In *The Projection of the Astral Body*, Muldoon and Carrington wrote

> Yes, you are using your astral body even now; it is tuned down, we might say, to harmonize with the vibrations common to material substance. Now there are factors which hold it down, and there are factors which tune it up. The powers which can be exerted to disharmonize the attunement are the powers which will cause the astral to move out of the physical. (p. 48)

If this is true, your soul is vibrating a few orders of magnitude higher than your body, but the two are in sync. It is as if you and your body are experiencing the same musical note, but in different octaves. This exercise will help you to raise your vibrations.

The exercise is as follows: Lie down, close your eyes, and relax completely. Imagine that you are separate from the body and lying inside the body-shell. Imagine that your physical body is vibrating slowly, and your astral body is vibrating at a faster rate. Pretend you can both hear and feel the vibrations throughout your astral body as if you were standing in front of nine-foot speakers.

Next, imagine the vibration of the astral body increasing in pitch gradually, getting higher and higher. As the pitch gets higher, the two notes go out of sync and a certain resonance gets stronger and stronger.

Repeat this exercise several times. This simple exercise can actually produce the vibrations that can separate you from your body. It also may help to try to listen intently for any sounds "inside" your head at various points in the exercise.

7

The Party

For me, the out-of-body experience was analogous to a party happening in a neighbor's apartment. Up to now, occasional psychic experiences had been like party noises; I did my best to ignore them. Dabbling with altered states of consciousness was like walking upstairs and putting my ear up to the door. The pokes and prods were like party noises I heard from outside. My first OBE was like opening the door and walking into the party. What happened next was like going in, getting drunk, and inviting everyone back to my place!

The day was November 26, 1979. Twenty-four days had passed since my first two out-of-body experiences of November 2. It had been two-and-one-half months since I started exploring altered states of consciousness, trying to learn about the OBE. My playing with altered states had shaken me up quite a bit because of the pokes, prods, sounds, and sensations I hadn't expected. My first OBE shook me up even more; it was undeniably real and made the pokes and prods seem trivial in comparison. Little did I know that my dabbling had opened some kind of psychic door.

I was living at home while attending classes at the university and working part-time. That day, my mom had a friendly, nonalcoholic birthday party, and JP and I started talking about OBEs. He asked me to try a quick experiment: he held up his right index finger about an inch away from the space between my eyes and asked me if I felt anything. I felt a strange sensation there, as if part of my astral body was being pulled out of my forehead. I tried to explain what I felt and asked him what it was. He said he didn't know for sure, but the space between his eyes worked the same for him. I hadn't read anything about the "third eye" yet, so I didn't pursue the matter.

After the party, I went to bed and made my nightly attempt to induce an out-of-body experience. After a few minutes of practice, I opened my eyes and saw movements and lights in midair! I was frightened, and to make matters worse, I started drifting away from my body! I panicked and tried my hardest to stay in my body! Once I was securely in my body, I closed my eyes and decided not to continue. I eventually managed to fall asleep, but much later than normal.

The next morning I woke up tired with the alarm clock. I had to get up early to go to my 8:00 A.M. class at the university. I realized I was too tired to pay attention in class, so I decided to get some caffeine in my system to help wake up. Since I hated the taste of coffee, I went to the refrigerator and grabbed a bottle of soda pop, opened it up, and sat down at the breakfast table. I took a sip and sat there trying to wake up and get motivated. Without warning I felt the bottle accidentally slip out of my hand and my hand closed into a fist. I was startled and expected to hear a loud crash as the bottle hit the floor, but there was no sound. I quickly looked at my hand, and the bottle was still there, securely in my grasp! It wasn't psychokinesis; my astral hand had accidentally "let go" of my physical hand, but the physical hand held tightly onto the bottle. I knew right then it was going to be a strange day.

I caught my usual bus to the university and went to my usual classes. My last class got out at noon, and I needed to be at an important meeting at work by 1:00 P.M. I debated whether to stop for lunch. Something deep down inside me said, "It's okay, you have enough time." The thoughts seemed to be my own, and yet separate from me, like a deeper source of knowledge. I dismissed it: "That's just my stomach voicing its hunger."

I walked over to a local sit-down restaurant. I looked at the menu. Their specialty burger looked great, but it was served with a small portion of potato chips. I was very hungry for french fries, but short on cash, so I ordered the burger "as is." After the waitress left I thought to myself, "I have enough money and I'm hungry; I should have ordered the fries. I really want the fries." I didn't want to bother the waitress by changing my order, so I didn't say anything.

A few minutes later, the waitress brought my burger with a large serving of french fries! "Something strange is happening here," I thought, "This is getting weird." Was it a psychic experience? "No," I thought, "it was just a coincidence."

When I was almost done with my lunch, that same "something" deep down inside me said, "You better hurry or you'll miss your bus for St. Paul and miss your meeting." Again I dismissed it, thinking, "That's just me, worrying about being late for the meeting." Nevertheless, I rushed to the end of my meal and paid my bill. I wasn't charged for the fries.

I ran across the street to the bus stop and my bus was just pulling up. How convenient! I got on the bus and looked at my watch. It was 12:15 P.M. The trip from Minneapolis to St. Paul usually takes 45 minutes, so I felt confident I would not be late for the meeting. Then it occurred to me: if I hadn't rushed through my lunch, I would have missed that bus, and I would have been late for my meeting. Was it a psychic experience? "No," I thought, "It was just a coincidence."

I wasn't late for the meeting, but the meeting kept me from working on an important project, so I decided to work late. I worked until 9:40 P.M. that night, then I went to catch my bus back to Minneapolis. By "coincidence" a bus pulled up almost as soon as I got to the bus stop. I got on the bus and sat down. I needed to catch another bus in downtown Minneapolis, so I got out my bus schedule and looked up when the other bus would be at my Minneapolis bus stop. The bus slowly pulled away from the bus stop and started sluggishly lumbering down the street at 15 miles per hour. My other bus was due to arrive downtown at 10:15 P.M. and the next bus after that was 11:40 P.M. The driver kept driving at 15 miles per hour for the next five city blocks.

Since it was 9:45 P.M., I only had 30 minutes to get to Minneapolis to catch my 10:15 P.M. bus, and it was usually a 45-minute bus ride. To make matters worse, the bus driver was driving 15 miles per hour! I started to get very discouraged. I was brooding. I thought to myself, "I wish there were some way I could make this bus driver understand that I need to be in Minneapolis by 10:15 P.M."

One block later the bus pulled up to the next stop and another passenger got on board.

Then something strange happened. The bus pulled away from the bus stop like a bat out of hell! The driver kept accelerating until he was ten miles per hour over the speed limit! He drove to Minneapolis at breakneck speeds—speeding the whole way—and passing up half of his bus stops! He even ran through a red light! He pulled up to my Minneapolis bus stop at 10:10 P.M. The trip took just twenty-five minutes, a new world's record! I got off the bus, and it tore off into the distance. "Wow!" I thought, "That's incredible!"

As I patiently waited for my 10:15 P.M. bus home, I thought to myself again, "Was it a psychic experience?" How many coincidences can pile up before you believe that something extraordinary is happening to you? If someone off the street, or even a respected scientist, were to tell me of a series of psychic experiences like that, I would have laughed in his face. But since they were happening to me, I couldn't laugh. "All right," I admitted to myself, "things like that don't just happen *by coincidence*. That's an excuse I've been using too long."

I had asked for out-of-body experiences, not psychic experiences. Somehow I had gotten them both. Somehow I was becoming psychic, whether I wanted it or not. I absolutely loved the psychic things that were starting to happen, but I started to worry about my sanity. What's next—delusions of grandeur? Psychotic behavior? Paranoia? Just how important are my thoughts anyway? Can this power be abused?

"Should I tell anyone what is happening to me?" I asked myself. "If the experiences had not been mine, I would never have believed them in a million years. So how could I expect anyone to believe they happened to me? No way!" I vowed not to tell anyone.

As a skeptic, I didn't want to believe in psychic experiences. I thought it was all a load of rubbish. But in the years ahead, as I kept practicing OBEs, I also kept having psychic experiences. Most days I would have three to five experiences I would classify as "psychic." They happened so often that I couldn't deny they were real.

I doubt that the psychic experiences were directly related to the out-of-body experiences. Rather, I think they were more related to the practice, during which I would induce altered states of consciousness. I discovered that when I became too wrapped up in daily life, I would have fewer psychic experiences. And if I took the time to meditate and explore altered states of consciousness, I would have more psychic experiences.

I was disappointed that many OBE books never mentioned the connection between OBE practice and psychic experiences. People brave enough to try to induce OBEs should be aware of the connection: when you try for OBEs, you may get more than you expect! Some of these psychic experiences can be alarming, unnerving, and sometimes even scary. I'll talk more about psychic experiences in chapter 25.

EXERCISE 7
Hypnogogic Play

Sleep is a very complex thing. Each sleep cycle has several stages, including the dream stage, or rapid eye movement (REM) sleep. Most of my out-of-body experiences occur during the hypnogogic and hypnopompic states. The hypnogogic state occurs at the beginning of the sleep cycle when we're just starting to fall asleep. During this state, the conscious mind is normally "letting go" and the subconscious mind is taking over. The hypnopompic state is similar, but it occurs when we are waking up naturally (i.e., not awakened by an alarm clock).

It's very easy to recognize these states of consciousness: in both states, it is normal and natural to see mixed-up visual images and to hear voices. Usually the voices and images don't make any sense.

For this exercise, I want you to experiment with these states of consciousness. Learn to recognize these hypnogogic images and watch them or listen to them with interest instead of falling deeper into sleep. Just "play" with these natural altered states to get a feel for this type of experimentation with the "borderland" of consciousness. This kind of play is fun, and can induce OBEs. Since we typically have five or more sleep cycles per night, we have at least ten opportunities to have OBEs every night! That's seventy opportunities for an OBE every week, in addition to your normal practice sessions!

As an experiment, try to stay awake or prolong consciousness while you're falling asleep. Try to "walk" the thin line between being conscious and unconscious. Try to get closer and closer to sleep while holding onto a thread of consciousness. Learn to hang onto that borderland state for long periods: this is a useful skill in learning OBEs.

Late one night I was using a computerized "TALK" program, talking to other programmers. I asked one guy what he was doing up so late. He said he has always had problems sleeping for as long as he could remember. He had a bad case of insomnia and hadn't slept for days. I told him I could cure his insomnia, and he said he didn't believe me, but he'd be forever grateful if I could. Well, I started telling him about my astral escapades, and I ended up giving him about five OBE-techniques to try. Several weeks went by. The next time I ran into him (on the same TALK program) he said, "It worked! You cured my insomnia! With your techniques, I fell right asleep! I haven't had any problem sleeping since!"

The point is, it's easy to fall asleep during OBE practice. The best way to keep from falling asleep is to rouse yourself as soon as you recognize the first signs of sleep. In this way, you can learn to hold onto consciousness without drifting off to sleep.

Another technique is to lie down and try to fall asleep with your arm held up in the air, bent at the elbow. When you start to fall asleep, your muscles will relax and your arm will drop, waking you up. This way, you can learn to get very close to sleep without being overcome by it. Later, you can stop holding up your arm during practice and get even closer to sleep while remaining conscious.

These exercises have another benefit. By doing them, you are learning to unite the conscious with the subconscious. You are learning to keep yourself conscious during the times when your subconscious is usually in control. And when that happens, your conscious can talk directly to your subconscious without interference. Then magical things will start to happen. Your subconscious will cooperate with your conscious. Your left brain will cooperate with your right brain. Your creative mind will cooperate with your analytical mind. All areas of your life will improve.

8

Overcoming Fear

Clearly, as long as I continued to try OBEs, strange and frightening things would happen to me. After some serious consideration, I decided that I had been playing with fire. This OBE business was just too scary and dangerous. What was it doing to my body? What was it doing to my mind? Was I becoming prone to outside forces, such as spirits? I had begun to worry about my sanity and started to wonder if I were some kind of freak. I decided to quit trying to have OBEs and try to go back to a normal life.

The next two weeks I didn't attempt any altered states of consciousness. I tried my best to go back to my normal life. But although I wasn't trying, weird things still happened to me. I started reading people's minds. I started to "know" what song would be on the radio next. As I was trying to fall asleep at night, I would still feel the same weird sensations: swaying, pokes, and prods, the whole gamut. It was even more alarming because I wasn't trying to make them happen.

I came to some important conclusions. First, there was no turning back—I couldn't just turn it off. Second, the best way I could deal with these weird experiences was to explore them and try to understand them. I needed to learn how to control them and how to control my fear of them.

I began by confronting my fears. As long as I feared these experiences, they had control over me. If I could eliminate the fear, the experiences would no longer have that power over me. I could be in control of myself and the experiences.

The first step was to organize my thoughts. I listed all the reasons why I wanted to have more out-of-body experiences and why I should not be afraid of them. The list looked like this:

1. I wanted to have more OBEs. After the first two experiences I couldn't turn away and forget it. I tried that and it didn't work. Besides, my curiosity still motivated me to go on.

2. I reasoned that someday, when I die, I will be forced out of my body, and I'll have to deal with the issue then. It seems better to learn the rules before I die, so I can handle it better when my time is up. If I explore the out-of-body state while still alive, perhaps my transition to the waiting world will be smoother. When I die, I will be cast into a strange new world, just as an infant is cast into our world. Imagine how wonderful it would be if a fetus could attend some kind of school while it was still in the womb! Imagine a baby that can talk on the day it is born!

3. When people die, they are all cast out of their bodies. It is our inevitable, inescapable fate. As billions of people have died since the beginning of

time, this new world must be quite safe for human "existence" and not as frightening as I thought.

4. I had been out of my body twice and nothing terrible had happened to me: I hadn't felt any pain, I hadn't been attacked, and there weren't any demons waiting to possess my body. During the first experience, I was gently floating in the air. I felt completely safe at the time. My fear of the unknown is what stopped both OBEs.

5. I had recently read several OBE books, some of which had hundreds of OBE narratives. In almost all cases, people described the OBE as beautiful, painless, and even ecstatic. Many people who experienced "near death experiences" (NDEs) didn't want to get back in their bodies. They were perfectly happy and content to stay out forever!

6. Despite my distrust of the Catholic religion, I still held some beliefs, such as a belief in God. I figured that if I were a good person, God wouldn't let anything bad happen to me while I was out of my body. "After all," I thought, "I'm dealing with God's kingdom."

7. The OBE books I read claimed the body is equipped with safeguards to pull me back into my body if things get too rough. The books said that many simple things would automatically bring me back to my body, such as poor blood circulation, fear, and thoughts of the physical body.

8. I believed (and still believe) in "guardian angels" who help me in times of trouble or need.

9. I also read that if I got into serious trouble, I would faint and my subconscious would take over, bringing me back to safety.

I read over my list and confronted my fears directly. I became determined to learn to face and control my out-of-body experiences and their side effects, even if it meant death. That night I wrote a note in my journal, explaining what I was doing and how I felt about death. I made my apologies in case I died during practice.

Once I faced and conquered my fears, I started attempting OBEs again. This time I took a more serious approach. I developed a simple training schedule: every Saturday and Sunday morning I would lie around in bed for several hours, trying to leave my body. I was no longer just dabbling with altered states of consciousness; I was on a mission. I was an explorer, determined to discover my own truths.

With practice, I got better at reproducing the conditions necessary to induce the vibrations. I learned to remain calm during my attempts, and I discovered that staying calm is very important.

All this OBE practice had other positive side effects. By trying to leave my body, I actually learned how to better control it. I learned to use my mind to control the persistent itches that always spoiled my attempts. This led me to discover how to block out pain with my mind. Eventually I learned how to use my mind to control sneezes, hiccups, and other bodily functions. The practice also taught me how to hold on to consciousness while driving, regardless of how sleepy I am, and how to fully relax under tense conditions, such as at the dentist's office.

I also learned that fear wears off over time. After you confront the unknown a hundred times, it's no longer as frightening. Conquering my fears was a big step in my spiritual development, and it made me a much happier person in daily life. It gave a whole new meaning to the famous quote from The Bible: "Yea, though I walk through the valley of the shadow of death, I will fear no evil." (Psalms 23:4)

EXERCISE 8
Resolving Fears

However frightening OBE practice might be, the actual OBEs themselves aren't frightening. They are usually very peaceful and happy—not frightening at all. OBEs are only frightening to people who don't understand what's going on. Mostly it is fear of the unknown. Being put into unfamiliar surroundings with new laws can be terrifying to anyone. But you don't have to be afraid of OBEs if you understand the rules.

Rule #1: Your beliefs create your experience.

Rule #2: Attitude makes all the difference. If you go into the experience with negative thoughts, your OBE is likely to be unpleasant. If you go into the experience with positive thoughts, your OBE is likely to be wonderful.

Rule #3: Your body cannot be possessed by a spirit while you are away. I'll say more about that in chapter 26.

Rule #4: There is no such thing as a "demon." I'll say more about that, also in chapter 26.

Rule #5: You can not get lost or lose your body.

Rule #6: The only thing you have to fear is itself.

The exercise for this chapter is as follows: Write down a list of each desire, belief, fear, and expectation you can think of. Of course, if you have a problem with writing, just running through it in your head will help.

First, write down your desires. Do you want to leave your body? Do you want to see higher truths? What do you want from this and other experiences?

Second, write down your beliefs about the out-of-body experience. Do you believe it is wrong? Do you believe it is a trick of the devil? Do you believe it is merely a dream? Do you believe there are demons or spirits out there to harm you? Do you believe hell and heaven are somewhere out there? Do you believe that demons or spirits can take over your body while you are out? Do you believe that the OBE is a sin in the eyes of God?

Third, write down your fears. Are you afraid of getting lost while out of your body? Are you afraid of spirits? Are you afraid of possession? Are you afraid of flying? Are you afraid of heights?

Fourth, write down your expectations. Do you expect to meet angels or spirits? Do you expect to meet other astral travelers? Do you expect to be weightless? Do you expect to be wearing clothes?

Fifth, go through your lists and mark each item you don't "like." For instance, if you believe demons can take over your body while you are out and that troubles you, mark that item. When you are done marking your "negative" items, go through each of them and confront them in your own mind. Don't attempt to have an OBE until your negative items are conquered or at least under control. Once you have conquered your negative feelings toward the OBE, your worries are over. If you still believe in demons, you might just meet one. If you don't believe in demons, none can bother you. But until you resolve these fears, your experiences may be influenced by them.

Examining and conquering beliefs isn't easy. I don't know of anyone who is completely free of negative beliefs. But working on them is a step in the right direction. And just knowing that you're working on them is usually enough to keep your OBEs wonderful and positive.

9

Scared to Death

After I conquered my fears about the OBE, I made good progress. My third and fourth OBE were self-induced, not sporadic. They were also short and uneventful.

Up until then, I thought there were only two ways to leave your body: through lucid dreams like my first two experiences or through practice like my third and fourth. It wasn't long before I discovered there were other ways.

01/01/80—OBE #5

. . . I was dreaming that I was camping along a riverside with a group of people. We thought we were safe, but suddenly two vampires—one male, one female—attacked our camp, and the dream turned into a nightmare.

I fought the female vampire for a long time and I finally killed her. I was exhausted.

Much to my horror, the other vampire came running and attacked me. We fought long and hard, but I was weak from my fight with the female vampire. He finally overpowered me and started sucking the blood out of me. I became weaker and realized I couldn't fight anymore. I was dying in my dream! I actually believed I was dying.

Then I woke up startled, and opened my eyes. I immediately saw a hand grasping for my throat! I was fully conscious, inside my body, and it seemed as if someone was trying to kill me!

I reenacted the dream-battle in my head for a few seconds, thought I was dying again, and I was ejected out of my body like bread out of a toaster!

I sat up and turned to look who was attacking my poor body. The hand that was reaching for my throat was my own! It was loosely draped over the pillow! I sighed a breath of relief. I wasn't in danger after all. I had literally been scared to death!

Although out of my body, I was glued to it. But this time, instead of trying to free myself, I tried to control my astral self with my mind. I thought hard, "I want to go to [my brother's house]" but nothing happened. Instead, I heard my physical voice (kind of muffled) saying it in the background! I looked at my astral hands. They were gently waving back and forth. . . . I was drawn closer to the physical body and I dropped inside and immediately opened my eyes (no blackout). I saw my hand draped over the pillow, as if it was reaching for my throat, exactly as I saw it during the OBE.

We've all heard the term "scared to death," right? Well, this OBE sheds new light on the term. Perhaps it shows there is no such thing as being "scared to death" because the worst that can happen is that you're scared out of your body. Perhaps it means we can only die when we are ready to die. I like to think that our deaths are planned by our higher selves, and there are no accidents.

In later OBEs, I discovered yet another way to leave my body. This one took me by surprise too:

Out of Body Experiences

05/23/80 Fri—OBE #16

I went to my math class. When class started at 12:15 P.M., something strange happened to me. I was sitting, and suddenly I became completely disoriented and couldn't feel my body. It seemed as if I fell out of my body and drifted to my left (west)! Then I came back and was disoriented and very dizzy. My dizziness wore off in seconds.

Since that OBE, I've had similar experiences in which I fell out of my body. Once I tripped and fell out while I was walking down the street! When I came back to my body, it was fine and hadn't missed a step.

The strange thing about this type of OBE is that it happens without warning, from full consciousness. I was in excellent health each time and not on any medications. I wasn't tired during the experiences, and my body wasn't very relaxed, at least not to the extent it normally is when I induce the vibrations. Perhaps we're not as body-bound as we think we are!

Some researchers have gone so far as to suggest that we aren't even "in" a body at all.[7] Perhaps our physical body is just a focus for our consciousness, and when we learn how to change our focus, we can leave the body at will.

---

[7] For instance, see *Out-of-Body Experiences*, by Janet Mitchell, chapter 8, entitled, "Whoever Said You Were in the Body Anyway?"

EXERCISE 9
Yo-Yo Visualization

This exercise uses imagination to create an astral swaying motion. Once created, you can latch onto the swaying, and it will pull you away from your body. I've used this method to leave my body several times.

The exercise is this: lie down, relax completely, and put yourself into a receptive mood. Next, imagine that there is a yo-yo in front of you at eye level. Imagine the yo-yo string is attached to the area between your eyes. The yo-yo is weightless, so it doesn't fall with gravity. A real yo-yo needs a pushing and pulling action from your hand, but this imaginary yo-yo needs pushing and pulling from your third eye. With your imagination, push the yo-yo down to the end of its string then pull it back to your third eye. As you work with the yo-yo, try to work your way into a single-minded, focused state of mind.

With your mind, push and pull the yo-yo about fifty times. Try to do this until your visualization is so real that you can actually see the yo-yo in front of you. Don't try to count the number of pushes you give, because that may unfocus your mind and bring you out of the single-minded focus.

You may think it sounds silly, but this is one of the most successful techniques I've ever developed. If you can't visualize it clearly today, keep working on it every day until you can. When you are trying to leave your body, there are very important key points to keep in mind, and one of them is realism. If you can visualize this yo-yo with absolute realism, out-of-body experiences are a short step away.

10

The Small Still Voice Within

One cold day in early 1980, I was waiting at a bus stop. At that time, I had about a dozen OBEs to my credit. I thought about my favorite television show, *Kung Fu*, which always had tidbits of wisdom sprinkled throughout the show. The Shaolin masters in the show were always portrayed as kind and humble, but above all, wise. I wished I could be wise like that. Then I remembered a story in the Bible about Solomon (1 Kings 3:5–13). In the story, God offered to give Solomon anything, and Solomon chose the gift of wisdom. Solomon was rewarded well for his choice. I wondered what it would be like if I were wise. "If I were wise," I thought to myself, "I could probably think up any question and look inside and find a truly wise answer there."

If I were a wise man and someone asked me questions, what would I say? I started to fantasize, asking myself philosophical questions and making up answers, pretending I was wise. Suppose they asked, "What is love?" I paused to think. I'd say, "Love is the binding force of the universe." If they asked "Who am I?" I would answer, "You are a spark of God's divine Light."

My bus wasn't there, so I continued with this day-dream. I asked myself more questions. Each time I'd look deeper into myself for the answer. After a few times I was surprised at the answers I came up with—they didn't seem like me at all! At the time, nothing seemed out of the ordinary, so I didn't even write about it in my journal.

This "wisdom game" was a lot of fun, so the next few days I practiced whenever I had free time. Instead of asking specific questions, I started asking myself to "say something wise." This also gave me unexpected results, such as:

Perfect love is never selfish. It's wrong not to love at all. It is better to love someone and selfishly desire their love. It is still better to love someone and desire to give them your love, asking nothing in return. It is best to love All That Is unselfishly and recognize everything as a part of that creation, including your loved one and yourself.

Upon closer examination, I didn't exactly make up words in my head when I asked myself questions. I got a jumble of thoughts, feelings, words, sounds, and images, and I "translated" this jumble into words. Then I said the translated words to myself, and somehow they made sense. Later, this translation process became so automatic that it was just like talking.

I had learned to ask myself questions and come up with answers, but I was very skeptical about it. It seemed as if I was pretty much "making up" the answers I wanted, even if the answers often had a lot more insight than I thought I had. The answers just came to me from the top of my head. They only came when I asked, and often they were the first things that entered my mind after I

Out of Body Experiences

formulated the question. For that reason, I viewed this all as a game I was playing, never taking it seriously.

Then the inner source of wisdom started to develop a personality of its own. Very gradually I started noticing that I was sometimes getting "answers" without asking questions. I started getting advice and reminders from within, that would come out of the blue.

I noticed that the answers addressed me in the second person; instead of receiving the message, "I should park over there," I would receive the message, "*You* should park over there, Bob." Also, the answers started getting more specific. Messages like "You should park over there" became "You should park over there because there's more time on that parking meter than this one." Later, these things turned out to be true. At first I thought I might be going crazy. Crazy people heard voices. But as I said before, I wasn't really hearing voices; I was just getting impressions and translating them into words. Then I began to worry about spirits.

So one day I decided to probe a little deeper into this issue. One day after I left work, I went for a short walk and started asking this "source" some new questions.

Q: What is your name?

A: You can call me anything you like.

Q: Do you have a name?

A: Names are not important; wisdom is important.
   Remember, the message is important, not the source.

Q: Are you a spirit?

A: No, not as you think of it.

Q: Then what are you?

A: Someone who has your best interests at heart. I am you, another part of you.

Q: Why are you here? Why am I hearing you?

A: My job is to help you in any way that I can, to help you become more aware, to see that you pay attention to the lessons that you are learning.

Q: If you're me, than why do you address me as "you"?

A: That's to help you tell the difference between your own thoughts and my messages.

Because of some book I had read, I started calling it my "inner voice." For months I distrusted my inner voice. Sometimes I would take its advice and sometimes I would not. Time after time, my inner voice proved its guidance was sound, but still I would not trust it. And because I was afraid of what people would think, I never told anyone.

One day my inner voice started speaking with me, saying, "Why do you constantly fight me?" I replied, "I just don't trust you; I've heard of stories where insane people murder and later say that 'God' or 'voices' told them to kill. If you ask me, any kind of nonverbal communication seems really strange to me; if anyone knew I talked to a voice inside of me, they would lock me up." My inner voice replied, "Have I ever told you to kill people? No! Have I ever told you a lie? No! Have I ever given you any reason to mistrust me? No! Has anything I've said ever been wrong? No!"

It continued. "Always remember this: it is okay to listen to your inner voice, and it is okay to take its advice, but always, *always* use your own judgment. You are not allowed to use *me* as an excuse for not taking action, or for taking an action, or for not using your own judgment.

As long as you use your own common sense and judg-ment, you aren't going to murder people, because com-mon sense tells you that murder is wrong.

"I am here to give you advice and helpful hints. I can give you answers to any questions, provided those ques-tions are not part of your current lessons. For some les-sons, you must find the answers for yourself.

"What I am asking is very simple. Try an experiment: try trusting me and taking my advice (while still using your own judgment and common sense) for one week, *without fighting me*. After one week, if I've lied to you or misguided you, feel free to ignore me. However, if my advice has been good, you can take this as far as you want."

I agreed to the experiment, and I started following the advice of my inner voice. One week passed and my psychic awareness increased. I decided I would continue to trust my inner voice until it gave me reasons to dis-trust it.

That was the beginning of a new cooperation between me and my inner voice: It started giving me more advice, helping me interpret my dreams, and reminding me of things I had forgotten. For example, one morning I got my motorcycle out of the garage to go to work when my inner voice told me to bring my bag of tools with me—"It'll come in handy today; you'll regret it if you don't." So I got off my motorcycle, walked back inside and got my tool bag. I asked my inner voice if my motorcycle was going to run into mechanical problems. It replied, "Your motorcycle is fine." "Then why should I bring tools?" "Trust me. You'll regret it if you don't." Later that day, as I pulled into a parking spot, I noticed a man with a stalled truck. I asked, "Having truck problems?" He said, "Yeah. You haven't got a Phillips screwdriver on you, do you?" I got out the tool bag and gave him a screwdriver. I was glad I had brought the tools, and I thanked my inner voice. It was right—I would have regretted it if I had not brought the tools.

My inner voice is often fond of helping people. For example, one day I went to my credit union, but I arrived ten minutes before they opened. I walked down the street, wondering what I should do to kill the time. Then my inner voice asked me to go into McDonalds, which was in the opposite direction. So I walked to McDonalds and went inside. The man in front of me ordered some coffee, but his speech was very slurred because he was deaf. The man repeated himself several times, but the cashier didn't understand. I knew a bit of American sign language, so I acted as translator to allow him to speak with his cashier. After I left the restaurant, I felt good inside. My inner voice congratulated me for a job well done.

My inner voice also provided me with "psychic" information I could not have known otherwise. One day I decided to eat lunch in the cafeteria. I stood in line trying to decide what flavor of yogurt to buy. Finally I decided to get blueberry yogurt, so I picked up a container. Then my inner voice said, "boysenberry." I asked my inner voice, "Do you mean I should switch?" It replied, "That's okay. Eat what you like." So I decided to keep my blueberry yogurt. I sat down and opened it, and there was boy-senberry-flavored yogurt inside! The carton was plainly marked "blueberry" and the carton was deep blue. But the yogurt inside was purple boysenberry.

My inner voice carefully guided my actions, and things always worked out to my advantage. This journal entry from 1985 shows what I mean.

More "psychic" events. About a month ago I found out that Boston (the rock group) had a member named Barry Goudreau, who put out an album. Since I'm a fan of Boston, I tried to find the album, but it was out of print. I went to every record store I knew in the Minneapolis and St. Paul area, but nobody had it. I told JO that I'd mail her a copy of the album on cassette tape if I ever found it. Well, I was going to mail another tape to JO today, and my inner voice was very active.

First I had to go to an office-supply store to find a mailer to mail the tape in. I went and found a perfect-sized mailer, and was going to buy one, when my inner voice said, "Get two!" I asked it, "Why? I'm not planning to send any more tapes for a while."

My inner voice, "Just get two; I'm sure you can find a use for the second one." I was in a hurry, so I didn't argue with my inner voice; I just bought two, without any plans to send another tape. When I went to the post office, I got the best parking spot, when *all* of the other available parking was taken. My inner voice had suggested before I left from home that I should make some copies of the latest MSPR [Minnesota Society for Parapsychological Research] newsletter. So after I left the post office, I went to the university to make more copies of the newsletter. As fate would have it, I couldn't find a parking spot except two blocks away from the print shop. My inner voice said, "Park here; it's not that far to walk." So I parked there, and started walking to the print shop. On the way, I noticed something interesting in a shop window, so I looked at the shop. It was a record shop, a very tiny one I didn't know about and one I'd never been in. My inner voice said, "Go in. The newsletters will wait."

So I went in. It was a very small record shop, but there was a section that said "ON SALE." My inner voice said, "Go over there and look in the "G's." I replied mentally, "Oh come on! I've hunted in every record store in Minnesota for Barry Goudreau's album; this tiny store won't have it, and they wouldn't have it on sale!" But I thought, "Oh what the heck, it doesn't hurt to look." Sure enough, I had been very carefully guided to find Barry Goudreau's album, and it only cost me $2.19! I told the shop owner that I'd been hunting high and low for that album, and had been to almost every record store in the Twin Cities, and couldn't find it anywhere. He said, "Really? That's interesting. And now you found it on sale."

Then I made the copies of the newsletter. I came out of the print shop and I remembered that I never fed my parking meter. My inner voice said, "Don't worry about it. Go over to JRCA and buy some tapes to record the album." I argued back, "But my parking meter is expired, and JRCA's tapes are not as cheap as Best Buy. I could go to my car, save myself a ticket, and get tapes at Best Buy for $2.00 each, whereas JRCA tapes are usually $2.50 each." But my inner voice insisted that I go to JRCA. Despite the fact that I always argue with my inner voice, it always knows what is best for me. I went to JRCA, and asked, "How much are your Maxell UDXL-II's?" The man went and grabbed four tapes. (I wanted to buy four tapes, but I didn't tell him that!) He told me the tapes were $1.99 each! I only had $9.00 left, so I had just enough money to buy four tapes! I got back to my car. No ticket!

My inner voice has been responsible for much of the "psychic" information I have received. In many ways, it seems like "cheating" because I don't have to work for this information; it's there for the asking.

I also found out my inner voice had a sense of humor. One morning I wrote down an out-of-body experience, and I lost track of the time. When I realized I was running behind, I left in a hurry. I bolted out the door when my inner voice suddenly interrupted, "Hey, Bob, you forgot to lock the door!" I ran back, locked the door, and thanked my inner voice. My inner voice jokingly replied, "You'd forget your body if it wasn't attached!"

I've also been helped by my inner voice during my out-of-body experiences. For example:

07/25/82 Sun—OBE #80

. . . I used the same swaying method to get out of my body again. . . . I was stuck to my body. I thought about it some more. I figured that the only way I could move was to close my eyes and trust my feelings. So I closed my eyes but immediately thought, "No! If I close my eyes, I might fall asleep!" If I have been reading for an hour, and I close my eyes, I will usually fall asleep. I knew this was very likely. So although I had started to move, I decided to open my eyes, and saw that I was again in the same place. I thought of another way: if I could change my vision to purely astral vision, I should be okay, I thought. So I lifted my arms out in front of me, and I tried to see clairvoyantly. I heard my inner voice clearly say, "Practicing clairvoyant vision here will greatly help your earthly clairvoyant vision." I looked at my arms, not astrally, but clairvoyantly, as if trying to see a spirit from the physical world. My arms looked like transparent, dark black, filmy shadows. I studied them for a while, then blacked out.

Here is another example of my inner voice helping me during an OBE:

10/31/82 Sun—OBE #83

. . . Another thing happened last night. It was like a lesson from my inner voice. It wanted to teach me the difference between clairvoyant vision and out-of-body vision. So first it showed me a place clairvoyantly, and it said, "This is clairvoyant vision." Then it showed me the same scene with out-of-body vision. I remember some of the differences. First, although both pictures were clear and vivid, the out-of-body picture had more of a sense of depth. I could tell my spatial location, because I had normal depth perception. In the clairvoyant vision, I saw the same things, and I could tell it was three-dimensional, but it was more like a photograph, where some particulars stood out more than others. In short, the clairvoyance was like looking at a regular photograph, except that some objects in the room seemed somehow emphasized. The out-of-body vision was different in that I was in the picture.

My inner voice has been one of the most beneficial forces in my life. Amazing things can happen if you begin using this tool. Your inner voice has always been there; all you have to do is listen inside.

What exactly is an inner voice? Some people may believe it to be a spirit guide. Perhaps some of today's "trance channels" are merely talking to their inner voice, then doing the same sort of verbal translation. Personally, I believe the inner voice is a communications link to the oversoul, or higher self.

My inner voice is notoriously honest and blunt. Once I asked it, "Why didn't you communicate with me before that cold winter day?" It replied, "Why didn't you listen to me before?" I asked, "Why don't you talk to me more often now?" It replied, "Why don't you listen to me more often now?" Then it struck me: Why don't we all?

EXERCISE 10
Astral Doorway

This is a variation of the OBE technique found in many books, such as *Astral Doorways*, by J. H. Brennan.

Get into a comfortable position and close your eyes. Relax as completely as you can, and start a visualization. Pretend that your consciousness shrinks into an infinitesimal pinpoint of light. Then visualize that you are standing in front of a locked door. Visualize the doorway any way you want, with fancy engravings and door knobs or whatever—personalize the doorway.

Next, visualize yourself taking a fancy key out of your pocket (or from a chain around your neck) and unlocking the door. Open the door and step through the doorway. Close the door behind you, and lock the door again. The symbolic act of locking the door is for protection: lock it every time you use it.

Put the key back where you found it, and start walking forward. Imagine there is a tunnel in front of you with a bright light at the end. Imagine that you walk to the end of the tunnel, step outside, and find yourself outside your body, standing next to it.

Next, visualize a complete out-of-body experience, in all the detail you can imagine. Imagine walking away from your body to a destination. Try to imagine and remember as much detail as possible. When you are done, imagine walking back to your body. Imagine finding yourself back in the tunnel, walking back to the door. Again, unlock the door, step through, and lock it again from the other side. Guide yourself back to full consciousness and open your eyes.

Many authors say that this exercise in visualization can induce genuine OBEs, as well as impressing the idea of OBEs on your subconscious.

11

The Clairvoyant

By the end of July 1981, I had had 44 OBEs, and psychic experiences were piling up. I was doing computer programming for the Minnesota Department of Natural Resources (DNR). One of my co-workers was LD, an ordinary woman except for her eyes. I couldn't look into her eyes because they seemed to look right through me. Somehow I got the strong impression she was clairvoyant. I talked to JP about her and he suggested I ask her. I didn't want to; she'd probably think I was crazy.

Everyone at work used a computer mail program, much like modern e-mail. One day I wanted to send a message to my boss who wasn't very prompt at reading her online mail. LD read her mail often, so I sent her a message that said, "Please tell PL [my boss] to read her mail." A couple of days later, LD sent me a message that said "This is not a message." When I asked her to explain herself, she complained that she never got any "good" mail. She sent me a noninteresting message because my message to her was so noninteresting. I got gutsy. I sent her the following reply:

FROM: BOB FRIDAY, JULY 31, 1981
9:39 A.M.

So you don't want messages like "Please tell PL to read her mail," huh? Okay. I always like a good philosophical discussion. I'll start it out with a bang.

ARE YOU CLAIRVOYANT?

Much to my surprise and relief, I was right: she *was* clairvoyant! She also had out-of-body experiences and was even attending a spiritualist church. Like me, she was afraid to talk about it for fear of what others might think.

LD and I became good friends. I rarely saw her in person because we worked different shifts, but we exchanged computer mail for a couple of years. During that time, we agreed on a little experiment: To establish proof during an OBE, I would try to visit her while out of my body. When I arrived, she could see me clairvoyantly and validate that my OBE was "real." From then on, I started trying to reach LD during my OBEs.

Literally all of the books on out-of-body experiences claimed that during an OBE everything is controlled by the person's thoughts. To travel, they said, all you have to do is to think of the person or place you want to visit, and you will be magically transported there. And I fully expected my thoughts to be all-powerful during an OBE, but I found out it wasn't that simple. The following excerpt from my journals illustrates some of the problems I had during OBEs, especially when trying to travel to a specific place. It also illustrates several points about OBEs, including clarity of consciousness and how out-of-body sight works. The topic of consciousness is discussed in chapter 19, and out-of-body sight is discussed in detail in chapter 18.

10/24/81 Sat—OBE #52

. . . I woke up at 8:00 AM. this morning and decided to try to have an OBE. I had no luck on my first try. I finally went back to sleep, and I kept going in and out of sleep until 9:30 A.M. I was fully relaxed and in the proper state of mind when I woke up the next time. I mildly thought about OBE, and I noticed how relaxed my body was.

I felt a twinge of vibration, and I directed my attention to it. It grew stronger, but it wasn't as strong as my first experience with the vibrations. It was more like the type I used to feel when practicing at night. "Well," I thought, "I wish I could remember what to do next, like I usually do," but I couldn't, and already the vibrations seemed a little weaker. Then I thought, "Well, I could arch my back, but it probably won't work." I couldn't think of anything else, so I decided to try it. I arched my back and threw my arms back behind my head. I was immediately flung into my astral body.

When I reached the peak of my backward (downward) motion, I started to sway back up again. When I reached my body again I made an effort to get away, but I got stuck to the body instead. I was fully conscious, glued tightly to my body, and amazed that my consciousness was so perfectly clear. Strangely enough, I could "see" all right. I had the astral equivalent of physical sight . . . I freed my astral arms, reached behind me, and tried to push myself away from my body. As I pushed, I felt my astral body being stretched from behind. I felt just like a cracker stuck in a vat of very thick honey. I felt millions of tiny streamers or ribbons attached to the two bodies (not with my hands; I just felt them there). Well, I gave it my best effort to get free, but I reentered my body after about 15 seconds.

So I came to, and thought it was the end. I rationalized that I couldn't do it again, because I was fully awake. But my stubborn side demanded that I try it again. So I got comfortable, and looked for the vibrations. They came immediately, and I used the same method to get out again. I wasn't stuck to the body this time. I sat up with no problem, again with a good sense of sight. I looked around and thought, "Wow. I'm really conscious. I've never been this conscious before. Not even in waking life. Now I'm going to do some experiments I've been meaning to do."

The first experiment that came to mind was to test how sound worked. So I said something like, "Hello? Testing one-two-three." Although I formed the words with my astral lips and used my astral vocal cords, no sound came out. I faintly heard a tiny voice in the background, but it was too muffled to understand. Perhaps the problem was merely my brain's interpretation of the sound.

Anyway, I looked around and noticed how things looked different in an OBE. In the past, I had often seen gray clouds during an OBE. But now I examined my sight more closely. I saw a few places where astral matter was just sitting in small bunches. And as I looked around the room, I noticed that everything was normal except that now I could see different types of "glows" around everything. It was as if everything in my room had an aura of its own, which glowed a little differently from any other thing. . . . I also noticed that in some places there seemed to be blots, or places where the aura was either black or covered up by a blackness. Then I thought to myself, "This is foolish. I am wasting my time. I should go at once to LD's house for purposes of verifying the reality of this experience." But then I blacked out again and once more woke up immediately in my body.

Once again my analytical self said no, but I was too stubborn to give up. I repeated the method, the vibrations came again, and I was ready for another excursion. When I got out, I was about one foot above my body. I sat up. I knew what I wanted to do: get to LD's house. I thought to myself, "Hmm. There are two possible routes I could take: through the back door or out through my window." I heard the back door open and shut, so I directed my attention to it. My astral vision opened up, and I saw my mom coming in the house. I also noticed the clock in the kitchen, but it was too blurry to see the time. It was more like second sight or clairvoyant vision than physical sight. I thought, "I'd better not go through the back door; there is too much risk of being distracted. You'd better try the window." So I looked at the window sill, then tried to go to it by pulling the image toward me. The image of the window did come to me, but when I looked again, I was still no closer to it. I tried to look at it closer. At once my eyes tried to be like a "zoom lens" on a camera. But instead of my eyes magnifying what I saw, I moved closer to it in a gliding motion. I had only glided one foot closer when I came to a stop. I tried to do it again, and it worked a tiny bit. Then I was about two feet away from the window sill.

I thought, "Enough of this moving-with-my-mind nonsense." I got up on my knees, then stood up, preparing to step through the window. I decided to keep my eyes open so that nothing could go wrong. As I stepped through the glass window pane, my consciousness dimmed considerably. At once everything seemed strange. I was outside, but it looked so strange that I couldn't tell where I was. I looked around and saw images, possibly from an oncoming dream. I couldn't even tell whether I was on the first floor or on a second story. I recognized things, but everything seemed out of place. I saw toys, furniture, and other objects. I twisted around and saw that I was outside, to the north of our kitchen, and one story up! I became confused and eventually blacked out. I remember thinking, "I don't want to enter a dream now." I woke up fully conscious in my body again.

I got comfortable and tried again. I immediately got the vibrations again as soon as I thought about them. Instead of flinging myself backward, I just flung myself forward and sat up in the astral body with no trouble.

I thought, "Almost every book I have on astral projection says that you can travel to a person instantly by thinking about them. I'm going to try it again." So I closed my eyes and visualized LD perfectly in every detail. I just sat there and visualized and nothing happened. I thought at first that my visualization wasn't good enough. But I had visualized her perfectly in every detail. I opened my eyes and I was still in bed sitting up in my astral body. I thought, "This is getting me nowhere." I started to think about LD, hoping this would work better than visualizing her. Still no results. Then I blacked out for maybe half of a minute. Then I woke up in my body again and knew it was over. . . .

This entry shows another unsuccessful attempt at travel:

04/10/82 Sat—OBE #70

. . . I couldn't see my arm, so I figured that I must be out of my body. But just to make sure, I reached my right arm down through my bed. When my arm went through the physical bed again, I knew I wasn't physical. I swung my legs around, pulled away, and stood up. I tried to walk but couldn't. I was standing about four feet from my bedroom door, with my arms outstretched toward it. As much as I tried to get away, I didn't move an inch. I thought, "My only hope is to think of LD and maybe I will be transported there." I closed my eyes and thought of LD. Nothing happened, so I visualized LD. Again, nothing happened. I thought of her personality. No movement. I imagined how I feel when I'm with her. Still no movement. None of this worked at all. I felt another quick motion, and I felt myself become physical again. I was totally back in my body again.

A few times I could "think" myself to another location, but these had unpredictable results:

07/10/82 Sat—OBE #79

. . . I closed my [astral] eyes and started thinking about LD. I opened them again and nothing had changed. I decided to try to visualize LD instead. I closed my eyes, and visualized LD. "LD," I mentally called. I opened my eyes and looked around. I was not in the same place! I didn't see LD either. I had no idea where I was. I was so overwhelmed by the change of scenery without any physical sensations, that I lost all consciousness. . . .

03/25/84 Sun—OBE #105

. . . I launched myself straight up in the air. I thought about LD and in a split-second, it seemed as if my consciousness blurred and instead of flying, I was transported somewhere at a blinding speed. That confused me, and I thought for a second, "No! I want to fly there." I felt LD's presence for a second, but my confusion sent me back to my body again instantly. . . .

11/10/85 Sun—OBE #118

. . . I pulled out and up so that I was in a squatting position near my body's right arm, about a foot up from the body. I knew right away what I wanted to do. I had read almost all of Robert Monroe's book, *Far Journeys*, so the first thing I wanted to try was to contact my guides—a process that Monroe calls, "ident inspect." The first thing I tried was saying aloud, "ident inspect," but nothing happened. Then I tried thinking, "ident inspect," and nothing happened. Then I heard the friendly thoughts of another person. It was a 30-year-old man's voice, and it said, "What are you trying to do?" I looked around, but I couldn't see anybody. I replied, "I'm trying to contact my guides." The other voice said, "Oh. But 'ident inspect'?" I felt very foolish and laughed. I must have looked pretty foolish trying to contact my guides by saying—or thinking—the words I had read in a book. Especially since the words were just the author's attempt at describing an indescribable astral experience. And especially since I was so incompetent at using my mind as transportation. "Never mind," I said, "It's from a book I read."

Then I tried to pull myself toward the "ident inspect" instead of thinking about it, but I lost all consciousness. The next thing I knew, I came to in my body a couple of hours later.

To people who live without bodies, we must seem like simplistic children. When we are out of the body, we must be willing to try new things, learn from our mistakes, and not be afraid or embarrassed to ask for help. Above all, we should be able to laugh at ourselves.

EXERCISE 11
Falling into a Well

As always, get into a comfortable position and close your eyes. Relax as completely as you can, then visualize looking down a very deep well. Next, pretend that you fall in, head first. As you fall, watch the bottom of the well getting closer. Try to imagine the sensation of falling as realistically as possible. Feel the gravity pulling you toward the bottom. Get caught up in the feeling. If this works, you may be zapped into your astral body. If it doesn't work the first time, repeat the visualization several times until it seems almost real.

12

Flight School

After reading so many books on out-of-body experiences, I had great enthusiasm about astral travel. After all, why hop a plane to the coast, when you can hop the astral plane to the ghost? But I tried everything I knew to travel with a thought; nothing seemed to work. Perhaps my expectations had been too great. Perhaps science had been too deeply ingrained in me, and a part of me still believed traveling had to be more complex than thinking.

Whatever the reason, I decided to take a different approach to out-of-body transportation. Instead of trying to use my mind to teleport myself, I decided to fly the friendly skies! My first attempt at flight wasn't too disastrous, but not too coordinated either:

01/27/81 Tue—OBE #32

... Some unknown time in the night I woke up out of my body. I could not see in the physical sense of the word, yet I knew where I was; I was in our back alley, and I knew I was [astral] projecting.

I thought, "Where should I go?" and immediately decided "to EJ"—I had decided this before I went to bed. . . . So I took a running leap and started off in the air.

I rose above the houses quickly and was shaky for a while; I remembered many flying dreams in which I had crashed. But I decided if I controlled my mind I would be all right. I flew higher and higher, and was touched by a little fear; I was afraid to fly too high. So I made an effort to keep myself low enough for my own comfort. I could see the roofs of houses, the trees, and everything.

When I first went up, I realized I wasn't seeing physically, so I thought, "I should see." Then I saw everything okay. I saw my arms raised in front of me Superman-style. I started to climb too high for comfort, and I became afraid of getting too far away from earth.

With that thought, I started getting lower and lower. I descended very quickly until I was forced to land. I landed okay in some street, on the slope of a hill. I thought, ". . . Now I'll never get there!" The next thing I knew I was dreaming again.

Nobody ever taught me how to fly, so I was proud of my first attempt. My next attempts at flying were just as awkward, if not more so.

05/08/82 Sat—OBE #72

. . . I walked through the door and outside. . . . It was bright and sunny outside. The change was striking to me, since the room in which my body was sleeping was dark. The sunlight didn't hurt my eyes; it just seemed very clear and bright. I thought, "Now where should I go to take off on a flight?" I looked up and saw the branches of our hackberry tree. I walked along our sidewalk toward the west.

I went to our front yard, and I stopped and faced the east. I looked all around. I was very embarrassed to be out in the public where everyone could see me about to take a flying leap in the air in an attempt to fly. I knew that I couldn't be seen by anyone, but still I hesitated, dreading the possibility that I might be seen. Such a flying attempt would look pretty silly for a physical person. I took a few quick steps toward the east and leaped forward into a good flying position. For a second or two I was completely weightless, and I glided in midair for a few feet. But then I stumbled and fell, catching myself before I fell on my face.

I decided to try again. This time I walked further west until I was on the front sidewalk outside our house. I ran about five feet toward the south this time (away from my house) and took a flying leap into the air, after looking around for neighbors who could see. I fell flat on my face again! It didn't hurt because I was not physical, so I picked myself back up. I decided to walk to our back yard (east) and try [to fly] there once. I walked about ten feet or so and blacked out without any warning.

07/02/82 Fri—OBE #77

Early this morning I was dreaming. I dreamed that I was talking to someone about astral projection. After the conversation ended, and I was back inside my bedroom, I said to myself (still in a dream state), "That's an excellent idea; I think I'll project."

So in the dream, I stood up and went outside. I walked to the place just behind (east of) my house and woke up there out of my body! I realized my condition, and I was surprised, but I stayed in perfect control of my emotions: the dream had prepared me to be calm for the upcoming OBE.

I was standing outside, facing east. I thought about recent failures with astral levitation, but I said calmly to myself, "It's worth a try." With an act of will, I started rising through the air, straight up, in an upright position (standing). It startled me but I told myself, "Stay calm; it's no biggie. I'm going to go for a nice, simple flying lesson. I'm not going to try for a big adventure."

I waited until I was about fifteen feet in the air, then I said, "Okay, that's high enough for now." The thought that I might not stop rising did cross my mind, and it caused me to rise a bit further, but I said to myself, "It's okay. Nothing bad can happen. I can't be harmed. I'm in control." So I stopped in midair. I totally relaxed my astral body so I couldn't even feel it, and propelled myself forward through the air toward the east with a mere thought properly placed.

I was slowly moving (flying) toward the east in a comfortable position. I thought, "I'm totally relaxed. This is a great bodily position to be in for flying." Then I looked down at my astral body, and I saw I was almost upright. My arms were hanging down, my head was forward, and I was leaning forward about thirty degrees. My legs were relaxed and naturally bent about forty-five degrees. The position I was in was almost exactly that of a ten-speed bicycle rider except I was more upright and my arms were relaxed by my side.

I wasn't too steady in my flying. I bobbed up and down, left and right, trying to correct my direction of flight. I was moving slightly faster now, and the ash tree in my yard was straight ahead of me. I tried to steer around it, but I could not; I wasn't practiced enough at flying. I was just about to hit the tree, when I wiggled my torso to the left (north) and my head managed to miss hitting the tree. The rest of my body hit the tree, and much to my surprise, it bent around the tree and slithered around it elastically like a snake overcomes an obstacle. "Whew!"

After that, there was nothing in my way. I started flying a little faster, and I purposely climbed higher and higher. I climbed to about four hundred feet, then I descended back to about two hundred feet, so that I could see the scenery more closely. I looked down without any panic at all and noticed that I could see everything well—equally as well as in the body—and very clearly. But I saw there was no sun, and I felt it was dark out. I could see fine, however, and everything appeared in a pale, almost gray light. It was like seeing a picture from an infrared camera.

I glided softly, somewhat slowly over the houses, eyeing the details of the neighborhood houses. I kept a close eye on all the details of everything as I moved, and verified that once again I was in a real, waking situation. The details didn't change, nor did my speed. And the tremendous detail I saw around me assured me I was seeing reality and not a dream. I reasoned that

1. In dreams I notice very few details, only those that are necessary to the immediate story unfolding around me. This wasn't a dream. Besides, I was fully awake and conscious.

2. Even in ordinary reality we screen out and ignore most of the details of our surroundings. So I knew I was experiencing reality with more clarity than normal, in-the-body life.

3. Since what I saw didn't change (I was looking for changes), I knew my eyesight was at least normal, and that I wasn't dreaming. Dreams have a bad

habit of changing the scenery to produce certain situations and emotions.

4. I verified and studied the details I saw below. The details were all the same as in waking life.

I flew to the east about three city blocks. I looked to the north and saw a man come out of a house that was on the north side of Lowry Avenue. He stood and looked at me, up in the air. So I brought myself softly down across the street, on the south side of Lowry, also to the west (I was now kitty-corner to where he was standing). He walked across the street toward me and came up to me. Just as he began to speak, I lost consciousness and entered the dreamlike semiconscious state. In this state, the man and I exchanged a few words, and I lost consciousness. He was about thirty years old, with short brown, wavy hair, very friendly, with kind eyes. He wore casual clothes. He was a little taller than I—perhaps six feet tall. I can't remember anything we said while I was in the dreamlike semiconscious state.

This OBE brings up a very important question: what's the difference between a lucid dream and an OBE? I do believe that occasionally people confuse one experience with the other. It's very difficult to tell the difference in some cases. Some people believe OBEs are poorly-developed lucid dreams. Others believe lucid dreams are poorly-developed OBEs.

A comparison of the two experiences is given in chapter 6 of *With the Eyes of the Mind: An Empirical Analysis of Out-of-Body States* by Gabbard and Twemlow (1984). The authors found the following differences between OBEs and lucid dreams:

Lucid dreams occur in 50 to 70 percent of the population, whereas OBEs occur in 14 to 25 percent of the population.

There are two types of lucid dreams. The first occurs during REM sleep, and they are known as dream-initiated lucid dreams (DILDs). The second type occurs at the beginning phases of sleep, and these are called wake-initiated lucid dreams (WILDs). Both types occur only during sleep or the onslaught of sleep. Typical OBEs are initiated from a waking state, much like WILDs are, but some OBEs unexpectedly occur from a waking state. Several people have reported OBEs during which they have unexpectedly "fallen out of their body" from total consciousness, as described in chapter 9. Some of these occur when the physical body is active, such as walking down the street.

Lucid dreamers can consciously program their dreams, whereas OBEers are usually passive observers.

Lucid dreamers have an integrated body image, whereas OBEers view themselves as separated from the physical body, which is inert and thoughtless.

Lucid dreamers have vivid, even mystical consciousness, whereas OBEers experience a more normal form of consciousness.

Lucid dreamers view their experience as a production of their minds, whereas OBEers view the experience as objective reality.

Lucid dreamers have brain waves typical of dreaming, whereas OBEers don't exhibit dreamlike brain waves.

Lucid dreamers have rapid eye movements (REMs), whereas these are not observed during an OBE.

Lucid dreamers typically don't see their physical body, but OBEers usually do.

In addition, the authors felt that fewer lucid dreams have a lasting positive impact on the subject, whereas OBEs usually have a highly positive lasting impact.

In a lucid dream, one typically does not dream about being in one's bedroom, as is common in the out-of-body state.

After a lucid dream, the subject accepts the "unreality" of the dream after awakening. After an OBE, the subject usually asserts emphatically that the experience was "real."

Many lucid dreams contain sexual content. In fact, author Patricia Garfield indicates that "fully two-thirds" of her lucid dreams have sexual content. Lucid-dream sex is convincingly real; it feels the same as real sex. OBEs, however, rarely have sexual content. When OBEers report having "astral sex," the experience is not anything like physical sex. It's more like an ecstatic mind-trip, a transfer of energy, or a euphoria, but it doesn't feel like physical sex.

Lucid dreams—like normal dreams—are not easily remembered, unless one is conditioned. Memory is a key factor of having lucid dreams. OBEs, however, are usually remembered vividly for years without prior conditioning.

Also, an out-of-body experience is a typical feature of a Near Death Experience (NDE). One can hardly think that lucid dreams occur during an NDE, especially because the physical body doesn't spontaneously go into REM sleep during an NDE.

Perhaps the most convincing argument is this: I've had lucid dreams in which I had complete control, then dispelled the dream only to wake up in an out-of-body state. When this happens I've noticed that the scenery in a lucid dream seems artificial, unlike OBE scenery. It's even possible to change the scenery with your mind. Here is an example:

09/17/86 Sat—OBE #126

This morning I was in the beginning of a dream in which I found myself walking through the hallways of a hospital, and there were other people in the hallways. I realized I was dreaming and became lucid.

First, I wanted to play with the lucid dream state for a little while, so I started gliding through the hallway. Then I levitated my feet and began to fly down the hospital corridor at a good speed. The hallway ended, but instead of hitting the wall I decided to change my focus and create a tunnel that I could fly down. With an act of will, a hole appeared in the wall ahead, and a tunnel formed. The hospital scene slowly blended into a tunnel scene, the hallway becoming the tunnel. In real life, a tunnel of this size (without lights) would appear to be darker toward the end of the tunnel. The dream-tunnel I created didn't seem to end, and it appeared lighter in the back and darker in the front. There was a strange kind of grayish light, almost like a fog, that obscured the end of the tunnel.

I started flying down the tunnel at a great speed, but I knew it was an illusion. I got bored with flying, so I slowed myself down, lowered my feet, and focused myself back in the hospital. I was in the same hallway. I turned and started floating myself back down the hallway in the opposite direction, turned left, and moved toward the main desk. Then I stopped completely and decided that I didn't want the illusion of the dream anymore.

I closed my eyes to unfocus from the dream. The dream scenery melted away and my vision went black. I was floating out of my body. Then I decided to have some fun, and I started flying wildly in all directions, doing loop-the-loops and having a ball. I turned about twenty loops of great size, just like a jet airplane, but was unable to open my eyes for some unknown reason. Still, the sensation of flying was a blast.

I was having great fun flying so freely, so I decided to try an experiment—to try to fly to the sun. I stopped and stood straight up. I reached up over my head with an imaginary line of force, and I kept reaching, trying to touch the sun with my line of force. When I decided that my line of force had reached the surface of the sun, I tried to "feel" what it was like at the end of the line. It really didn't feel any different, just a little "denser" (that's the only way I can describe it).

Then I started pulling myself straight up, along that line of force, toward the sun. I accelerated tremendously toward the sun until I was traveling what I felt to be near the speed of light. After about three minutes of this tremendous speed I still didn't feel any change, so I stopped and tried to see where I was, but I wasn't able to see anything. With that, I blacked out and woke up inside my body.

If I had remembered any astronomy from my childhood, I would have known it takes more than eight minutes traveling at the speed of light to reach the sun. And I might not have been traveling at the speed of light.

The difference between the out-of-body experience and the lucid dream is not always apparent. I guess you'll have to rely on your own sense of "real" and "not real" to decide this for yourself. One thing is for sure: more scientific study is needed. It is premature to jump to the conclusion that "OBEs are actually variant interpretations of lucid dreams," as proposed by Stephen LaBerge in chapter 9 of his excellent book *Lucid Dreaming*.

EXERCISE 12
Lucid Dreaming

Many OBE experts say that some part of our psyche is already familiar with the out-of-body experience. Many books claim that every night some part of our psyche leaves our physical body and goes about work of its own. What happens then is so far removed from the physical world that we usually remember only bits and pieces of these journeys as "dreams."

During OBEs and lucid dreams your body is asleep, but unlike dreams, your consciousness is awake. Well, your body goes to sleep every night. Suppose you had a way to "wake up" your consciousness but leave your body asleep. You could turn an ordinary dream into an OBE. You could wake yourself up and say, "Wait a minute. I know this is a dream. I'm wide awake now." From there, you could either keep dreaming and have a lucid dream, or wake yourself out of the dream and have an out-of-body experience. Both are fun.

Lucid dreams are great. You literally can do anything you want. You can remain completely conscious and do anything you can imagine. They're almost as much fun as OBEs, but they're not as real. The scenery will be fake. OBEs, on the other hand, are sometimes more constraining, but they're real.

The problem is, when you're dreaming, you usually don't think to wake yourself up. In fact, you usually don't realize you're dreaming: you think you're awake.

Here's a simple exercise to help you get around that problem. Ask yourself in all seriousness, "Am I dreaming?" Well, are you? Maybe you're just dreaming about reading this book. So how do you know you're not dreaming all this? I want you to make sure you're not dreaming this.

If you ask yourself this question every fifteen minutes today, you'll probably ask yourself the same question tonight when you're dreaming. Daytime habits often carry over into dream habits.

You don't have to ask it every fifteen minutes, but the more often you ask, the more likely you are to catch yourself dreaming. You can set yourself a reminder, like your watch. How often do you look at a clock? Every time you look at a clock, try to figure out if you're dreaming. It won't take long. And it could be a life-changing experience!

So happy dreaming. And perhaps, happy OBEs!

13

"Ever the Silver Cord Be Loosed"

My first strategy for contacting people from the out-of-body state—using thought power—didn't seem to work. My second strategy—flying—didn't work well either; some distraction always stopped me before I reached my goal. I decided to try a third strategy, walking—at least until I could find a better way to travel. After all, what could go wrong with walking?

That's when I discovered the "silver cord" the books talked about. Most books call it the silver cord, based on a verse in the Bible (Ecclesiastes 12:6). The cord, they said, connects the astral body to the physical and will pull you back inside in case of danger. I soon found out the cord doesn't play fair:

03/08/80 Sat—OBE #11

. . . I jerked myself out of line of my body and floated up. I tried to get away from my body by clawing the atmosphere and using my legs to push. I got about five feet away from my body when the cord's pull became stronger and started pulling me back toward my body.

I fought the pull and about one foot away from my bed, I resisted the pull for a few seconds, and then was violently sucked back into my body by my cord. After I was rejoined to my physical body, I woke up and looked around.

I wasn't in danger, or even emotional during the whole OBE, and yet the silver cord pulled me back in the body against my will. Why?

Sylvan Muldoon and Hereward Carrington tried to address the cord-problem in their book, *The Projection of the Astral Body*. They claimed there was a "cord activity range" which is like a fifteen-foot magnetic field all around the physical body. If you're within the cord activity range, they said, the silver cord is likely to pull you back inside. However, once beyond that range, you are free to roam.

I was fairly angry with my silver cord, but what could I do to keep it from pulling me back to my body? Many books on astral projection warned me against tampering with my astral cord. They said if I damaged the cord, my body would suffer great physical harm, and if my cord was broken, my body would die.

But what made them the experts? How often have people actually tried playing with their astral cord? I decided to be cautious about it, but not cave in to fear and occult superstition. Rather than accept my limitations, I decided to fight back!

07/30/81 Thu—OBE #44

. . . My cord started a gentle tug back, but I responded immediately by resisting and, with a swimming-like motion, propelled myself forward in a southeast direction through the corner of my bedroom and into our kitchen hall. I walked into the kitchen against the tug of my own astral cord.

After struggling all the way to the kitchen, I got very angry at walking with the cord tugging against me. I turned around and grabbed hold of the cord and yanked it with all my might, to make more slack. The cord drooped down to the floor and I continued. . . .

In the experience above the astral cord seemed like a glowing piece of garden hose. I soon found out the silver cord can take different shapes, especially when the astral traveler is a somewhat disoriented computer programmer.

01/31/82 Sun—OBE #63

Last night I stayed up watching a television show until 1:00 A.M. I was very tired. This morning I woke up early once, and went back to sleep.

I started to dream. I dreamed that there was a party going on at our house. Then I woke up. The only things I remember from that dream were that (1) JP and CA were outside when the dream ended; (2) my bedroom door was open; and (3) LD and some others were upstairs in JP and CA's bedroom.

I drifted back toward sleep, but then I realized that I could project very easily; all I had to do was to throw my consciousness forward, and start astrally swaying. I was lying on my right side. So I pushed my whole conscious-ness forward. At once I was zapped into my astral body, and I started swaying forward and backward. The vibra-tions built until they were noticeable but were getting constantly stronger. I knew I was now partly in and partly out of my body. . . .

On a forward swing (or sway) I lunged forward and twisted up to separate the two bodies in a very sudden and violent manner. In my astral body now, as I made the movement, I felt a great tearing sensation coupled with the feeling that my solar plexus had just dropped, and I felt a bit sick to my stomach.

I was not seeing, but once again mind sensing. I was in a horizontal position about a foot above my body, pointed perpendicularly away from my body and about a foot away from the bed. For a second I worried that I might have torn my astral cord and made a permanent projection (death). Then I thought, "Well, it's too late to worry about it now. Either I'm okay or the damage has already been done." So I ignored it and decided to try to contact LD.

I was groggy. I noticed that I seemed to have a computer printout in my hand, and I felt the need to take this printout with me and show it to LD. I still had that last dream in mind. My bedroom door appeared to be open, although the physical door was really shut. And I somehow believed that LD was upstairs in JP and CA's bedroom. So I took the end of my computer printout and walked into the dining room. I didn't want my computer printout to tear, so I walked very carefully and turned to see how it would unfold itself. The other end was sitting on the floor next to my bed—apart from my body.

I walked backwards and watched it unfold and grow longer with each additional page being unfolded from the main pile. Upon looking back into my room, I saw the printout but no astral cord, so I realized that the unfolding printout was my astral cord (in disguise)! That's why there seemed to be no end to it! It only took the appearance of a printout!

I tried to climb through the ceiling into their apartment but was unsuccessful; I blacked out.

How's that for taking your work home with you? Anyway, since my astral cord didn't break during that experience, I decided not to be so "gentle" the next time I was out! No more Mister Nice Guy!

02/06/82 Sat—OBE #64

. . . I was in my astral body, swaying. I struggled, and pulled away [from the body] a little bit, but I felt the resistance of my astral cord.

Last night I had been conditioning myself for these problems. I kept saying the following affirmations to myself:

1. When I am in my astral body, everything is governed by thought, whether conscious or unconscious.

2. Nothing on earth is solid to me, except in my mind.

3. I will feel no resistance, nor any restriction of my freedom.

4. I will be able to go wherever I wish without interruption.

5. I should be able to see through walls and ceilings.

Well, now I felt the resistance of my astral cord, and I thought, "Hey! This isn't fair! I am projecting and I should be free!" But just then I was violently sucked back into my body after having resisted as long as I could. I woke up in my physical body after a short blackout, and without any ill effects.

I said to myself, 'I'm not giving up that easily!" and I tried the same procedure. It was relatively easy this time, and I slipped right out. I pulled away from my body on purpose and started walking toward my bedroom door. This time I could feel my astral cord taking up the slack and exerting a greater force. I was three feet from my body on the bed, upright and facing my bedroom door.

When I felt my cord starting to tighten, I turned around and faced my body. I'd like to note here that I was only mind sensing during the whole projection. And since I was not "seeing," I had to feel where my cord was. I felt it, and it was now joined to my astral self at the bottom of my rib cage, or just a little below my heart, and between where the ribs divide going down.

The cord itself felt smooth but very rigid, like a piece of garden hose. The cord was about one centimeter in diameter.

Anyway, I put my hand just above my cord, so that I would see where it was when I woke up. I somehow thought that my physical hand would be moved to that spot too. I got into a kung fu stance with my weight mostly on my back leg. I was now prepared to play tug-of-war with my own astral rope!

I yanked at the cord as hard as I could. I started resisting its pull, and I kept trying to reassure myself that I should, by all rights, be free from this menace.

I resisted the cord's pull for a little while, as long as I could, and then I got sucked back into my body again.

Apparently my kung fu stance didn't help me resist the cord any better. The cord held up against my most determined effort to pull on it, without any damage.

There has been a lot of discussion about the astral cord, what it is and whether or not it exists. Many people who have had out-of-body experiences or near death experiences have reported seeing a cord or cable linking their astral body to their physical body. People from all societies and all parts of the world have reported seeing a cord regardless of location, age, and religious beliefs.

Just as many people don't see any silver cord, even when they look for one and even when they expect to see one. I've had OBEs in which I have seen a cord and ones in which there was apparently no cord. I personally believe that the astral cord exists only as a psychological comfort or point of reference. I don't believe it has any actual connection with the physical body. Also, I don't believe it has any function, except as a psychological symbol.

I don't believe that playing with the silver cord can damage the body, nor do I believe that the body will die if the cord is severed. However, I caution you against such antics, just to be safe.

EXERCISE 13
Black Box Visualization

Here is another visualization exercise: Get into your favorite OBE practice position, close your eyes, and relax as completely as you can. Let yourself fall deeper and deeper toward sleep until you are consciously watching hypnogogic images.

Then visualize that a black box, about three inches on a side, is sitting three feet in front of your eyes and slightly to the left of the center of your imaginary viewing screen. Hold that visualization for about thirty seconds.

Next, visualize a cloud of gray, about the same size, sitting to the right of the box. The cloud has no definite shape, but it is taller than it is wide, looking almost like a snowman. Visualize the two figures side by side for another thirty seconds.

Next, visualize a thread of light slowly reaching from the black box to the gray blob. It reaches closer and closer until it reaches the gray blob, filling it with light. If you feel any strange sensations, remain calm and follow your impulses.

If nothing happens, repeat the visualization again from the beginning a few times. Make sure you do it slowly and as vividly as you can.

What in the world does this do? Well, I once used this visualization to leave my body. During the visualization, I felt a sharp sensation along my spinal column, and I got the urge to physically throw myself backward into the bed. I followed the impulse and tried to throw myself backward, but only my astral body moved, and I was out of my body. It was a very easy OBE. I don't know how or why it worked, but it did.

14

A Helping Hand

M y third travel strategy, walking, was as unsuccessful as the first two strategies. The silver cord and other things kept me from my destinations, and I was very disappointed. Nevertheless, I wasn't ready to give up.

Then, during one of my longest OBEs, I got brave and tried another strategy. I reasoned that the residents of the OBE-world should be more adept at traveling than I was. And since I wasn't having much success at traveling by myself, I decided to ask someone for help.

Until that time, I was content to explore on my own. I was afraid to contact "spirits" because I wasn't too sure of their power and what they could do to me when I was "out."

07/25/82 Sun—OBE #80

. . . I was completely out of my body. . . . I opened my eyes. I seemed to be stuck to my physical body. I tried to use my arms to turn myself around and get away from the body. And although I felt I was turning, my eyes told me I wasn't moving at all. I looked carefully and I was still in the same position. It was like being dizzy—I seemed to sense motion (spinning) but I wasn't going anywhere. I thought about this for a little while. I thought for a minute about what I should do to get away from my body. Then I blacked out.

I came to in my physical body, totally conscious, but in a very good condition for projection. I decided to try again. I used the same swaying method to get out of my body again. I tried to push my midsection up and down until I felt a slight tingling of the vibrations, then I tried physically to do the same thing. I gathered momentum by swaying, and I was pulled by it out of my body.

I separated from my body, only to discover I was stuck to my body again. I thought about it some more. I figured that the only way I could move was to close my eyes and trust my feelings instead of my eyes.

I closed my eyes but immediately thought, "No! If I close my eyes, I might fall asleep!" If I have been reading for an hour, and I close my eyes, I knew this was very likely. So although I had started to move, I decided to open my eyes, and saw that I was again in the same place.

I thought of another way: if I could change my vision to purely astral vision, I should be okay, I thought. So I lifted my arms out in front of me, and I tried to see clairvoyantly . . . I looked at my arms, not astrally, but clairvoyantly, as if trying to see a spirit from the physical world. My arms looked like transparent, dark black filmy shadows. I studied them for a while, then blacked out.

This time I woke up separate from my body, but inside it. I was surprised at that, and was very happy to still be out of the body. I seemed to be freer now than before. I walked over to the north wall of my bedroom after sitting up, without even noticing the physical things in my way—my stereo cabinet and my computer terminal and cabinet. I planned to go outside through the wall and then fly to LD's house.

I bent forward and stuck my head through the wall. I was looking outside. It was lightly raining, but it was hardly noticeable. Every previous attempt at walking through that wall had not worked, so I tried something different—keeping my head outside, I jumped up in the air, and did a somersault through the wall, and landed outside on my feet. I was free!

I walked to the back yard. I was preparing to fly, but I wanted a clear flying path. The ash tree was once again in my way. I walked near it, and then I jumped up and flew to one of its limbs. I was perched on an ash tree limb. I saw the apple tree next door, and some other trees. I thought, "How stupid of me to try to go through the tree. There are just more trees. I could have just walked to our alley and taken off there." But now I was up in a tree! I looked down. It was a long fall. I was afraid of jumping from that height! I considered the possibility of flying to the apple tree. I was just about to try it, but then I blacked out once more.

I was unconscious for a little while—maybe fifteen to thirty seconds. Then I woke up again. I was still out of my body! This experience was not unlike the first two. I was curious about that clairvoyant vision again. I held up my arms again and studied them carefully with clairvoyant vision. I was able to alter my vision so that I could totally see my astral hands as solid, not transparent, but I had to focus on them intently to see them this way. I experimented with that clairvoyant sight for awhile, then I lost consciousness again.

I was unconscious again for a short time, and I woke up once more out of my body! I was free again, and I rejoiced! I went over to the north wall again. I bent over and did another somersault to get outside. I got a brilliant idea then: "I'll call for help from guides!"

No sooner had I done this than I felt the presence of a very advanced, great being. I couldn't see him, but I felt he had a very large aura. I figured that I couldn't see him because his vibrations were much higher than mine.

He called mentally and two of his spirit friends came. These two friends, I felt, were less developed than the master whose presence I felt. They were servants of that powerful being. They weren't bound to him, but they always did what he asked, because serving him was their way to advance themselves spiritually. He told his friends exactly what to do. I didn't hear them exactly, but I could tell he instructed them to accompany me to LD's house.

The two friends were normal-looking spirits that were my own size. And I could see them all right. They were very friendly to me, and we became friends right away. These two spirits were average-looking men. One had brown hair, and the other had slightly lighter-colored, sandy brown hair. They were happy, and they were good friends. The "master" spirit left. Unfortunately I blacked out.

When I woke up again, I was still out of body. The three of us were walking east on Larpendeur Avenue toward Snelling Avenue. The two friends were talking. I tried to memorize pieces of evidence that I could look for later to prove the experience was "real," but I forgot them all.

After we walked for a little while, I suddenly felt a pain. I felt sick to my stomach and weak. I had an urge to go back to my body. I didn't want to fight the feeling. I knew I had to get back to that body. I stopped them and said I was sorry, but I had to get back to my body. They were very understanding about the whole thing. One said, "Sure thing. Take it easy, okay?" So we exchanged our goodbyes.

I faced east and closed my eyes. There was no lapse of consciousness; I saw complete blackness for a little while. I woke up out of my body again! I got up and thought, "How strange! Why did we bother walking—why didn't we just fly to LD's? This time I should fly there. Walking is way too slow." I stood up, and this time I blacked out. I was unconscious for a while.

Then I started dreaming. I dreamed I was having an OBE, but it was very obviously a dream, and not a real OBE.

EXERCISE 14
Imaginary Music

This exercise comes from a friend, JH. He used this exercise to leave his body:

First, get comfortable and relax as much as possible. Then choose a song you know very well. As vividly as you can, pretend the song is playing. Try to focus your complete attention on the music you are listening to in your imagination. Practice this until it seems as if the music is really playing. Again, try for as much realism as possible.

JH says when you can imagine the music clearly, the music can easily turn into the vibrations, and you can easily escape your body.

Some people are better at using their imaginations with sound rather than pictures. Try both and see which works best for you.

15

What Astral Programmers Do in Their Sleep

Many books on out-of-body experiences, especially those of occult origin, say that we subconsciously leave our bodies and do "astral work" during sleep. The trouble is, they usually don't say what astral work is, except maybe helping people with their "final transition," death.

My first OBE, with the split-consciousness, showed me that parts of the psyche can be very active during sleep. But I never considered myself an astral social worker by night. That is, until the morning of Tuesday, September 1, 1981, when I had my 46th OBE.

Sometime after midnight, I unexpectedly woke up out of my body. When I awoke, I was standing next to my bed in the middle of my bedroom. I was a bit surprised, but before I could gather my wits about me, I was "put under" by my subconscious. It felt as if I were knocked out by a professional anesthesiologist.

A while later, I woke up out of my body a second time. Again, I was standing in the middle of my bedroom.

This experience was also cut short when I was "put under" by my subconscious.

It seemed an hour or so passed. Then, just as in my first OBE, I slowly started to become more conscious, and I was aware of having multiple consciousness. My awareness increased until I was fully conscious, but this time my conscious self was an observer. I was allowed to watch with astral vision, but I wasn't in control. Another part of me was running the show, doing some very serious work, and knew all the tools of the trade. What I saw was astounding.

I was gliding slowly up from below, until I saw what looked like a human brain. I could sense the body it belonged to. Somehow, I knew it was my own body. The brain looked like about one hundred small spheres of light, grouped in the shape of a human brain. Each sphere had a different brightness. I noticed that four particular spheres were shining brighter than the rest, and I knew they had been cut off from the other spheres. Using my mind tools, I worked for about ten minutes adjusting neural pathways, "rewiring," and manipulating energy. Then I recharged the four spheres with energy. Next, I programmed the brain so that it would use different neurological connections and make automatic adjustments! I was a psychic healer in my sleep!

Satisfied with my work, I left. I approached a second brain and followed the same process. I rewired, transferred energy, then programmed the brain to aid in the healing process. After I was finished with the second brain, I worked on a third and then a fourth.

The fifth brain was a much more difficult case. As I approached the brain, I could tell that it belonged to a forty-year-old woman with dark hair. Like the others, she had some physical problem, and I sensed many damaged parts of her body.

I went through the same sort of procedure. I looked at the brain and saw many messed-up spheres. I sensed that she had stopped using certain parts of her brain until she had lost the use of these spheres. I pulled myself very close to those spheres as if I were looking through a magnifying glass and began to work. I worked for about an hour on her, "rewiring" and opening pathways. I transferred a lot of energy to her. My energy spread throughout her body, healing as much damage as possible. Then I spent a long time programming her brain to heal her body. As I left, her body and brain were both busy with the healing process.

As I approached a sixth brain, the observing part of my psyche began to gain more control. As this happened, I was poured like a liquid into my body. As I came to, I was in complete awe. I looked at my clock and saw it was 2:00 A.M. I went over the experience several times in my mind so I would not forget. Then I drifted off toward sleep.

At once, I saw another brain. Then my subconscious realized that "I" was consciously tagging along again. It quickly went back to my body, and I woke up again. I dozed off again, and this time I was out cold. My subconscious didn't take me along this time. The next memory I have is of dreaming sometime later in the night.

This OBE taught me many things. It taught me that sleep is not "idle" or "wasted" time. It taught me the importance of helping people and the importance of work. It was a humbling experience that gave me a great reverence toward my higher self.

Some portion of our psyche leaves our bodies whether we like it or not, and devotes a great deal of time and energy to astral work. Perhaps sleep is necessary to our survival and sanity because we need this subconscious astral activity. It's up to us to choose whether to be conscious and learn from the experience or to remain unaware.

EXERCISE 15
Moving the Pinpoint of Consciousness

I've used this exercise to escape my body a few times.
It can also induce other weird but harmless effects.

Close your eyes and spend a few minutes relaxing as
completely as you can and clearing your mind of all
worries and idle thoughts. Then spend a few minutes
trying to decide where your consciousness is seated.
Is your consciousness in the center of your head, or
perhaps somewhere between the eyes? Wherever it
is, visualize a tiny pinpoint of light at that point. You
don't have to be exact about the location.

If you're not comfortable with where you have visualized the pinpoint of light, move it until you are
comfortable with it. Spend a few minutes visualizing
that pinpoint of light as clearly as you can. Try to
shrink your awareness until you are only aware of
your head. Then shrink your awareness even further,
so that you can't feel anything except that pinpoint
of light.

Next, visualize the point of light slowly moving down
toward the base of the brain, where the cerebellum
is. Move it about four inches down, then slowly move
it back to its original position.

Repeat this visualization several times. This visualization can induce the vibrations and get you out of
your body.

16

To Believe

The "brain fixing" incident taught me an important lesson. When I was trying to prove my experiences were "real," I had problems achieving my goals, and I was usually disappointed. When I just let myself flow with the experience, I had fun and felt good about the experience. Suddenly I realized that I didn't need to prove anything to anyone. There truly *is* a higher purpose to our experiences, whether in the body or out. All that matters is that we believe in the magic within us and trust that we will be guided to what is best for us.

I never did make it to LD's house in a fully-conscious OBE, but I had some close calls. For instance, on October 4, 1981, after a fully-conscious OBE (#51) had ended, I entered a semiconscious dream state in which I was at LD's apartment. I took note of several details, including a pile of clothes I saw sitting on a bed. After I described the experience to her, she said it sounded "actually quite like our apartment. Especially the part about the clothes. I had done wash and put them on the extra bed." Eventually LD changed jobs, and I lost contact with her.

Since I made the decision to "go with the flow," I haven't been disappointed. My goal—to make my presence known during an OBE—also came with time and patience. In 1985, I had the following OBE during which my roommate, JH, was aware of my presence.

09/07/85 Sat—OBE #116

JH (my roommate) and I were discussing OBE last night until 2:00 A.M. after watching a horror movie on television. We both decided to try having OBEs, and we agreed that if either had an OBE, he would try to contact the other in the OBE state.

I first woke up around 7:20 A.M., and I thought about trying to have an OBE. I was very tired and fell asleep before I had a chance to try.

I woke up next around 9:30 A.M. and I thought, I've almost wasted the whole morning and haven't even tried to have an OBE." So I decided to try to have an OBE. I got into a straight position with my arms at my sides. I let myself approach sleep, but then I thought strongly, "I want to have an OBE." So I started by visualizing a line of light (about three feet long) going straight up from between my eyes. I reached out with my consciousness to the end of the line, and pulled myself toward the end of the line. Then I created a rocking or swaying sensation by pulling and then pushing my consciousness along this line toward its end. Almost at once I felt the vibrations sweep over me, but they were very mild—almost unnoticeable. The vibrations faded away after a few seconds, and I was separate from my body.

My eyes were open, and the first thing I tried to do was look down. I tried to turn my head down, but although I had the sensation of my head turning, my vision stayed where it was, staring at the upper corner of the bedroom. My mouth was very dry and stiff. My vision wouldn't move. I had a slight feeling of dizziness as I turned my head down, but my vision stayed the same, so I stopped.

Then I noticed some sort of spirit form gliding from the direction of JH's room, into my room, and I thought it was JH. I thought, "JH beat me here! Good! Now I don't have to go into his room to get him. I wonder if he'll remember doing this." The spirit figure I saw glided up next to me and came to rest to my left, near the bed. I turned my eyes to the left to look (I could not turn my head), but I couldn't make out the spirit figure too well.

As I studied the ghostly figure, another spirit form glided in and joined the first. As I studied the two figures, their forms started fading in and out, so that parts of them were completely transparent, parts of them were visible but translucent, and parts of them were completely visible. I could see now that neither of them was JH. One of the spirits was a man and the other was a woman, and they grasped each other while they reclined on the bed, less than a foot away to my left. They didn't seem to notice me at all.

I wondered if the images I saw were really spirits, or if they were thought-forms, or just afterimages from a time when two such people occupied the same room years before. I was strangely calm and not alarmed at seeing the spirits. Since the spirits didn't seem to care about me, I turned my attention away and concentrated again on trying to get away from my body.

I reached behind me, and tried to pry myself away from the physical body, but again I had the feeling of movement, although my sight remained the same. I tried to say some words, like "I am projecting now, so I should be able to get away," but the words seemed to come out physically. And since my throat was very dry and stiff, the words came out slurred together, as if my whole mouth was deadened by novocaine. I made a mental note to remember all of this and let myself back down into my body.

I looked around once more, and as I looked, many other spirits started fading in and out of my vision. I concentrated on seeing them, and as I looked, they became clearer in my vision, and soon it seemed as if the whole room was crowded with spirits of different kinds.

Most of the spirits were between the ages of thirty and fifty, and they were talking to each other in this crowded room. It reminded me of a dance or a wedding reception because there were many people crowded together, talking to each other. I moved my eyes back and forth, to scan the different spirits in the room. As I moved my eyes, the spirits seemed to move too, and it caused a strange effect. I was curious as to why, but it didn't bother me.

I studied some of the spirits in the room, and I remember what some of them looked like. One was a man about thirty-five years old, wearing '50s-style formal clothes, with some scratches and bruises on his face. He was talking to a woman, dressed also in a '50s-style formal dress. None of these spirits seemed to notice me either, so I decided to ignore them and try to get away from the body again to contact JH.

I lay back into my body and then I tried lifting my feet over my head to do a backward somersault, thinking that it should work, since it has always been successful in past OBEs. Again I felt my consciousness move completely in a circle. I quickly came full circle and found myself back in the same position lying down. My consciousness faded into the same dream I had before I woke up.

After awhile I realized I was dreaming again. I forced myself awake and woke up still out of the body. I thought, "I am out of my body, and I am controlling this reality entirely. I should be able to get away from this body." I decided that the only way I was going to get anywhere was to close my eyes and walk, relying entirely on my other senses. So I closed my eyes and bent my knees down until my legs were through the bed and my feet were touching the floor. I used my arms and a kind of swaying motion to stand up. I took a few steps toward JH's room. Then I stopped and wondered whether it would be better to walk into the living room, and through JH's bedroom door, or through the physical closet.

I decided to walk through the closet and straight into JH's room. So I kept going toward JH's room and approached JH's bed. Just as I started to look around, I was picked up and forcefully pulled back to my body.

The next thing I knew, I was back in my body, and my eyes were closed. I felt as if I were still out of my body, only I felt very stiff and rigid. I forced my eyes open, and as I did that, I became more physical, until my physical eyes opened and I was again completely in my physical body.

I turned to look at the clock, and it felt great to be able to turn my head. The time was slightly after 10:00 A.M. I recalled the whole incident in my mind. Then I got up to type it into the computer. JH heard me get up and came out and asked me if I had had an OBE.

JH said that he was experimenting with the hypnogogic state when he saw me in his bedroom. Other people have felt my presence too.

I am a believer and a skeptic. I must believe in the paranormal, since I've experienced it firsthand. At the same time, I am still skeptical in many ways. Skepticism is healthy because it can keep us from losing touch with reality and going off the deep end. We shouldn't believe everything we hear or read, or every line of trash fed to us by cults. We must always believe in ourselves, but question what doesn't makes sense.

The difference between a skeptic and a believer is simply this: perspective. When I was a skeptic, I approached everything with a negative attitude. I was a pessimist. Everything was hogwash until it was proven to be real. I thought of psychics and mystics as frauds, liars, and charlatans who lived lives of delusion.

My psychic experiences—particularly my OBEs— changed my attitude from negative to positive. I see people as inherently good. Obstacles are merely lessons to be learned. My outlook on life is positive and optimistic. And it pays to be optimistic. I believe in magic because I have experienced it firsthand.

EXERCISE 16
Quiescing the Mind

In my opinion, the *single* most important factor in leaving the body is that you focus your consciousness down to a single, focused, barely noticeable thread.

The best way to explain this is with an analogy. Imagine two parents who have lots of small kids who make lots of noise. At night, the parents send their kids to bed and wait for them to fall asleep before doing adult things. They try to be covert, so they listen for the noise in the kids' bedroom to quiet down, and when it does, they proceed. The lack of noise implies, but doesn't guarantee, that the kids are asleep.

Similarly, I think we all have a higher self or oversoul that waits until our consciousness is completely quiet or quiesced. At that point, it goes on to do otherworldly things.

I have found that if I narrow my consciousness down into a single thread (where my mind doesn't wander), and if I can hold my consciousness that way for about three minutes, the vibrations will rush in and start the separation process.

After a certain point where the vibrations have run their course, I broaden my consciousness back to normal, and I allow my normal thinking process to continue. But only after I'm in a fully conscious out-of-body state. It feels like sneaking through a security door with someone, unnoticed.

It's not enough to be single-minded. You have to narrow down your consciousness until it's almost unnoticeable even to yourself. It's also not enough to concentrate your mind. Concentration is different from quiescing your mind.

Here's an exercise for focusing your consciousness down to a quiesced state. Have you ever seen a flash of lightning and stopped to listen for the thunder? At such a time, you tend to stop thinking and listen. Your mind is quiesced for a second or two. Pretend that some sound will occur in the future, and just listen for it. For a short time, your consciousness will stop all processing and go into a quiesced state. As you practice, increase the length of time you listen.

Instead of being a thinker, try to be a listener or an observer. Don't think; be. Don't concentrate. Well, pretend you're staring at a blank screen in front of your eyes. Become passive, patiently watching and waiting.

At first, you won't be able to suspend your thoughts for long. With practice you can learn to prolong this passive state.

When the vibrations hit, it can be quite shocking and may break you out of the quiescent state of mind. If you start to think, "Oh my God, what's happening to me?" or "What should I do next?" then you've lost the quiescent state temporarily and the vibrations will start to fade away. Luckily the vibrations take several seconds to fade away—just enough time to recover the quiescent state. Just concentrating on the vibrations getting stronger is not enough—they will only get stronger when you get back to the quiescent state of mind.

Learn to hold your quiescent state of mind regardless of what is happening to your body. After the vibrations come, you need only hold the quiescent state for approximately 10 to 15 seconds and then you can just get up and walk away from your body.

Part II

What the Books Didn't Tell Me

17

What the Books Didn't Tell Me

As I began having more out-of-body experiences, I naturally set about doing my own type of scientific experiments. In my travels I encountered some peculiar things that weren't mentioned in the many OBE books I had read. Other peculiarities were only touched on by these books, but not explained to my satisfaction. Here are some of my findings:

Getting Stuck to the Physical Body

The first undocumented thing I ran across was the problem of getting "stuck" to my physical body. In several OBEs I found myself seemingly "glued" to my physical body, unable to move away from it. A typical instance was my third OBE:

12/09/79 Sun—OBE #3

. . . I was partly out of my body. My left arm was free. I waved it back and forth and looked at it to make sure it was really happening, and I wasn't dreaming. I tried to move more of my limbs, but they wouldn't budge. I tried to use my free left arm to push the rest of me out, but the rest of me was secure. (I couldn't move my physical or astral legs. They were cataleptic [paralyzed].) I felt that if I put my left astral arm back in its physical counterpart, I would leave the astral state. But being almost paralyzed, I had no other choices. I waved my left arm again, and looked at it, to once again make sure I wasn't dreaming. Then I returned it to its physical counterpart. That brought me back to the physical world, and I came to.

After some experimentation I found a few ways to "unstick" myself and pry away from the physical body. A good example is given below.

01/22/83 Sat—OBE #88

. . . My first problem was . . . to get away from the physical body that usually claims some sort of hold on my astral counterpart. This time I had no problem: I turned over so that I was face down (my body was face up). Then I pushed myself up until I was on my hands and knees. My hands, knees, and legs were still in coincidence with the physical body. Then I just withdrew my limbs one by one, and climbed off the bed. I was free from the body.

Most OBE books agree that out-of-body "reality" is mostly governed by thoughts, fears, and expectations. In one OBE, I used my fear of falling off the bed to counteract my expectation of being stuck, thus freeing myself.

Despite my limited success, I still haven't found a satisfactory solution to the problem of getting stuck to my body, but I do have a word of consolation: this happened to me more often when I was first learning how to consciously get out of my body. As time went on I had fewer experiences of being stuck.

Getting in the Body Backwards

This has only happened a few times, but it's an interesting experience when it happens. The first time this happened I was at my parents' lake cabin in northern Minnesota. I was feeling a bit under the weather, and I was tired. I went into my bedroom to lie down for a bit. I was lying flat on my back with my head to the west and my feet to the east. I induced the vibrations and floated about three feet above the body. My astral body seemed completely paralyzed and I had no control at all:

09/21/80 Sun—OBE #23

. . . I tried to go up, but I couldn't. I wanted to go forward, but couldn't. Finally I wanted to turn around, and I rotated so that my astral head was above my physical feet and vice versa. I started going down into my body the wrong way! Try as I might, I couldn't stop it. Finally I went into my body and blacked out for a second. When I came to again, I was disoriented; I thought I should be facing east like my astral body was, but woke up facing west in my physical body. In one instant I was in my astral body, looking at the west wall of the room. The next instant I opened my eyes and saw the east wall. I felt intensely disoriented, which was like a dizziness, but it seemed more physical than mental. In other words, it seemed as if I were still physically feeling the spinning or reorientation of my astral body. About one minute later, the dizziness went away and I felt normal.

Since no harm ever came from these incidents, "getting in" the wrong way was never a problem.

The Blackout on Exit and Reentry

Many books on the out-of-body experience claim that when a person leaves his or her body, there is usually a split-second blackout. The same blackout happens when the person reenters the body. What is this blackout, why does it happen, and what can we learn from it?

The split-second blackout that usually precedes and follows OBEs is a great concern because it may make the experiences seem more subjective and less objective, less "real."

Skeptics may say that the blackout suggests a loss of consciousness during which the person might actually start dreaming. They would say that the blackout is some kind of shortcut to the delta brain wave state that accompanies our everyday dreams. Therefore, they would say the OBE is just a dream, with only subjective reality.

Some theories claim that the blackout is necessary. Crookall believed the blackout is caused because neither the physical nor astral body is available as a vehicle of consciousness during the transference of consciousness. Some people believe the blackout happens because only the subconscious self can separate the soul from the body; therefore, the consciousness of the individual must give up all control to the subconscious during the transference. Others maintain that the blackout occurs because during the actual separation process, the physical brain is unable to interpret the experience. Or, perhaps the brain can interpret the experience, but for some reason or another, the portion of the brain that is responsible for memory is unable to function.

Despite the theories, I have experienced OBEs in which there was no lapse of consciousness during the separation process and OBEs in which there was no blackout during reentry. The first time this happened was on my fifth OBE.

01/01/80 Tue—OBE #5

. . . I looked at my astral hands. They were gently waving back and forth. I thought my waving must be interfering with my travels. I slowed myself down. It felt as if I was drawn closer to the physical body. I felt more physical. Then I dropped into my body and immediately opened my eyes (no blackout). There was no split-second of unconsciousness. I was fully conscious the whole time. I gently floated down into the body and felt myself become more solid. I immediately took charge of the physical body and opened my eyes, wide awake.

In my 54th OBE, I was fully conscious for the entire exit and reentry.

10/31/81 Sat—OBE #54

. . . I got really comfortable and started to "mind-sway" myself gently. I was extremely relaxed, and my mode of thought was perfect: *passive*.

I went deeper toward the unconscious state, but I never got there. I felt a strange electrical type of sensation one third of the way up my spinal column. I also became alert, and at the same time I became restless. I was on my back but my back was curved around my pillow, and I felt uncomfortable with that position. I turned over so that I was on my stomach, but I felt that my body didn't move with me! Only my astral body turned! I didn't let this bother or excite me, because I knew that the separation process was not finished. I knew I was half in and half out of my body.

I also knew what I had to do next to finish the process. I gently and carefully pushed myself down a little bit, away from my body; about one inch of me was out. I instinctively knew that the vibrations would come to me then. Sure enough, the vibrations came filtering down into my head from above. When the vibrations were at their peak, I took that as my cue and lifted out of my body, twisting at the same time so that I was heading for my bedroom door. I mentally noted how clear my consciousness was again. When I got to the bedroom door, I looked and realized that my astral self was curved around an astral pillow, just like my physical body was curved around its pillow. I reached over with my astral right hand and tried to pull the pillow away. That is when I noticed that I was dressed in the same clothes as my body—my pajamas. I pulled on the pillow, but it wouldn't come free.

I got frustrated and turned so that I was facing west. I was going to look at my body to the northwest, but I stopped turning when I looked to the west and saw some lights. I tried to look at the lights and study them, but I noticed that my sight was strange. Everything looked as if it was tilted back forty-five degrees—as if my astral body was leaning at a forty-five-degree angle. I wanted to see those lights better, so I tried to right myself. But no matter how hard I tried, I was still at a forty-five-degree angle. It was as if I was halfway between lying down and standing up. I thought to look at my physical body, but when I thought about my body, I immediately went into it without getting a chance to look at it.

I was now semi-physical in my body, and I made a great effort to stay awake. I kept saying to myself, "I will stay conscious." Then I thought that if I opened my eyes again it would help me stay awake. So with a great effort, I opened my eyes and everything was blurry. But I was awake. Then it seemed as though I was in the cataleptic state. Very, very slowly my sight became more "real" until I was fully back in my body. I was fully physical again. When I rolled over and looked at the clock it was 9:35 A.M., so I estimate the projection to have started around 9:30 A.M.

Here is another example.

09/18/82 Thu—OBE #81

. . . Then the vibrations swept into me, and I was cataleptic. I tried to move, but I couldn't. I struggled to get away from my body, but I couldn't. I opened my eyes. I could look around, but could not pull away from my body. My astral body was obviously separate from my body, and it felt free. I felt weightless, and yet I couldn't move. After trying to roll out of my body to the right unsuccessfully, I looked at my bookcase. I looked around some more. Then I tried to roll out to the left. Then I noticed a blur of red to my left. It was my clock, with a digital red display. I had heard that some people believe time moves differently while out of body, so I tried to look at my clock. The clock was just barely out of my field of vision; my body was pointing straight up. So I tried to turn my head.

After a great deal of effort, I managed to turn my head to the left. It was very hard to turn. But as my head turned, my whole being solidified. I was turning my physical head. With no break in consciousness, I felt my whole being getting bound into my physical body. By the time I finished moving my head, I was no longer astral, but I could see the time: 9:30 A.M.

I've had many more fully-conscious exits than reentries, for a simple reason: I usually try to make my OBEs last as long as possible, so I don't let the experience end until I black out or lose consciousness.

We may never know why the blackout usually occurs. Perhaps science will discover the reason, but not until the OBE is given serious scientific research.

Pain During an OBE

I have learned some interesting things about pain while I was out of my body. All the OBE books said that during an OBE, it is impossible to feel pain. They said only the body feels pain. So I was very surprised when I had the following experience.

04/26/80 Sat—OBE #14

I entered my astral body and suddenly felt a pressure at my astral rib cage on both sides, as if someone were poking me there! I couldn't stand the pain, and I twisted and put myself back into my body. Once in my body, I felt all right.

I left the body again, and the same thing happened! I tried to ignore the poke-pressure, but was overcome with the pain and had to go back again.

I was determined. I tried again. I swayed my astral legs once again. This time I noticed something strange. I didn't use my eyes or my astral eyes, but I could feel my astral limbs with my mind! I could also see them partially with my mind's eye, just like visualizing a thought! This time I also noticed my astral arms. When I got out, I wiggled my fingers. Again, I felt the tickle-pain in my rib cage on both sides. It wasn't as bad this time, and I also did a better job of ignoring it and withstanding the pain. I felt a hand grab my right wrist. It gently tried to help me away from my body, but once again the pain-tickle took its toll and I had to return to my body. When I came back to my body for the third time, I suddenly became very dizzy, and had to abandon the attempts.

This experience was the only one in which I felt "pain" in the true sense of the word. As I described, it felt as if someone was poking me in the rib cage very hard.

I didn't get around to actually experimenting with OBE pain until 1983:

01/09/83 Sun—OBE #86

. . . I clapped my hands in front of me as hard as I could. This made a sound, just as I had expected. I had hit my hands very hard, and I felt the pain in them for a second, but the pain was a painless pain! I clearly recognized the sensation of pain in my hands, but I swear it didn't hurt!

I've experienced this painless pain or mock pain several times. For instance, instead of floating up above my body on one occasion, I decided to float down under my body:

04/27/80—OBE #15

Sometime this morning I found myself conscious out of my body, but very near it. My first instincts were to get away from it. So when I thought about getting away,

I drifted down through my bed underneath my body. I could feel the bed as I went through it.

What I experienced was the sense of thirty or forty bed-springs piercing through my astral body as I went down beneath my body. The sensation wasn't painful, but I did feel the dull, throbbing sense of mock pain.

In another OBE, I very much expected to feel pain, but I didn't:

05/25/84 Fri—OBE #109

I woke up astrally. I had been dreaming that something was attacking me on my left side. I woke up (in the astral body) and found myself swinging my right astral arm, wildly hitting at the imaginary attacker on my left side. Although I was hitting my left side as hard as I could, I didn't feel any pain at all. I became fully conscious and continued to swing my arm, but only to gather momentum to swing away from my body. Soon I blacked out.

The subject of astral pain (especially the unexpected *lack* of pain) may very well be another way to clearly tell OBEs apart from dream states.

Making the Body Move During an OBE

The books I read on out-of-body experiences led me to believe that it was impossible to move the physical body during an OBE. I found out that it might be difficult, but possible.

Several times I have apparently forced my body's eyes open during an OBE, yielding some interesting results. I have written more about that in the next chapter.

Although I have no way to prove it, I have apparently made my body move in other ways during a few OBEs. For example:

11/08/80 Sat—OBE #25

. . . I started myself astrally swaying again. I tried moving my feet, and my physical ones moved! They felt very heavy. The foot I moved was not the swaying astral limb, but the physical one, and I could sense it move with my mind-vision. Just about then I blacked out and came back.

I have also apparently made my body speak during an OBE. For example:

10/04/81 Sun—OBE #51

. . . I was really in my astral body again, stuck to my physical body. I tried to say, "It's just not fair," but I couldn't! So I tried to telepath it, and I heard it faintly in my inner hearing. Disappointed that I couldn't "say" it physically, I tried very hard again. Then I heard my physical voice say it, but the voice sounded distorted, as if someone said it for me. Or as if the transition from the physical sounds to the astral sounds made it sound squeaky and distorted.

I've also had OBEs during which I've put all my energy into trying to make my body speak, without success. Again, only scientific experiments can prove whether a person can affect his body during an OBE.

OBE Myths

There are many myths about the out-of-body experience passed down through the ages, many of which cause people unnecessary concern.

State of Health

Some books on OBEs say that OBEs are easiest when the subject is in perfect health. Other books say that OBEs are easiest when the body is physically weak, sick, or exhausted.

I've had OBEs in sickness and in health, for richer and for poorer, for better and for worse, till death do I part! Most of my experiences were done in good health, but as a rule, my body's state of health hasn't affected the experiences or my ability to induce the experience.

Lying on Your Stomach

Many books caution the reader not to attempt an OBE while lying on their stomach. At first I had some concern about it, but the concern was short-lived.

04/05/81 Sun—OBE #38

. . . I rolled over onto my stomach. I headed off to sleep. I wanted to project, but I was too lazy to make any effort. I was almost asleep when I found myself waving. I thought, "Good. Now I can project." So I increased the waving. I was almost ready to come out of my body when I thought, "Wait. I read that you're not supposed to project while on your stomach. Maybe I shouldn't." Then the waving slowed down. I thought, "Maybe I should turn over." Then I thought, "No! That might ruin the whole attempt. I should take the opportunity while I still have it." So I started waving again. The waving got big enough, and I went up out of my body.

I've projected many times while lying on my stomach and never had any problems or discomforts from doing so.

Attempting to Have an OBE with Your Legs Crossed

Many OBE books caution their readers against attempting to have an OBE with arms or legs crossed, or with the body in any unusual positions. Supposedly, there is a danger of blocking the flow of energy in the body, which could possibly harm the physical body or astral body. Some books claim it's difficult for the astral body to leave the physical body in strange positions.

I've left my body in many unusual and awkward positions, and there have been no bad side effects.

It is important that your body be comfortable and relaxed during OBEs, and if you are comfortable and relaxed in an awkward-looking position, don't hesitate to use it. I would, however, recommend using only positions that allow good blood circulation. Some people look like a squashed ant when they sleep or like an airman whose parachute didn't open on time. My general rule is this: if you can sleep in such a position, it is safe to leave your body in that position.

Some positions do make it easier to leave the body. I've found that when I lie on my side, I am sometimes too comfortable and therefore fall asleep instead of leaving the body. When I lie on my back, it seems easier to control my state of consciousness.

Use of Energy During OBEs

I've often had people ask me if I came back to my body feeling drained. Not surprisingly, several books on OBEs claim that the experience requires a great deal of energy, and is therefore rare and difficult to achieve.

My experience has been just the opposite. I've never come back to my body feeling drained of energy. Rather than being tired, I return to my body feeling refreshed and happy. When I return to the body, I'm often exhilarated because the experience was so exciting and uplifting.

Although there have been many myths and legends about the out-of-body experience, there is still much to be learned. There is only one way to break through the barriers of fear, superstition, and prejudice that keep us from broadening our knowledge and expanding our consciousness: that is to test the myths, explore our outer limits, and bring that information out in the open.

EXERCISE 17
Head Rocking

Sit up straight (do not lean back), close your eyes, and very gently and slowly start nodding your head "yes." Don't analyze any of this; just try to feel that rocking sensation. Memorize that feeling of gentle swaying. Pretend that your whole astral body is also swaying just like your physical head is swaying.

There is a point where your head is balanced front to back, and if you nod your head with your eyes closed, you will probably lose that balance and feel slightly disoriented.

Do this several times at different practice sessions, spending at least a full minute each session. As a variation, try moving your head in small circles instead of nodding.

This exercise is good for many reasons. First, it will get you used to the feeling of being disoriented. OBE exercises can sometimes leave you disoriented, and becoming familiar with that feeling makes it easier to handle. Second, if you memorize this feeling of rocking, you'll be able to trigger the pre-OBE state more easily, which may have its own rocking sensations.

18

Fight for Sight

Scientific experimenters were quick to discover that OBE eyesight is different from physical eyesight. They set up a simple experiment. They placed an object inside a locked room. The subject was supposed to fly into that room and identify the object. The experiment sounds easy enough, but the subjects had problems identifying the objects. The most proficient subjects, such as Ingo Swann and Keith ("Blue") Harary could make drawings of what they saw during OBE experiments. Often the drawings were unrecognizable, or at best distorted. For example, in one experiment part of the "target" was an American flag. Ingo Swann made a very impressive and accurate drawing of the target. However, the flag was drawn as a rectangle with a box in one corner and stripes on the rest of the rectangle. Swann seemed to see the flag with some clarity, but was unable to identify it as an American flag. Why do such distortions exist?

In an attempt to tell whether some sort of clairvoyance was involved during OBEs, parapsychologists devised an ingenious experiment. They built an optical box that was computer-controlled. The computer would choose random colors, quadrants, and patterns. The colors and patterns were displayed in the chosen quadrant. The displayed image could only be identified if the subject was standing in a certain position in front of the box, where he or she could interpret the superimposed images as a single image. The complexity of the superimposed visual images was meant to rule out clairvoyance. This experiment had a very small rate of success, but sometimes the target was "seen," as if the subject was actually viewing the box from outside his or her body. But this experiment also had many problems with the eyesight being distorted. Again, why is this?

I believe the distortions in astral eyesight are partly due to the fact that the astral body isn't equipped with eyes that process light. Astral eyes are more for appearance than function. Therefore, the physical brain is forced to give physical interpretations to nonphysical "images." Many of my experiments were devoted to exploring the astral equivalent of eyesight.

The Different Types of Sight

I've experienced four basic types of sight during my out-of-body experiences. I call them astral sight, body sight, mind sensing, and clairvoyance. Of course, there is a fifth category: no sight at all. OBEs can sometimes be very difficult to describe because during the experience you may have switched several times among the four types of sight. One moment you might be mind sensing, and the next minute you use your astral sight to look at a particular object, and so on.

Astral Sight

Astral sight is best explained as the astral equivalent of physical sight. A good example is OBE #52 in chapter 10. This type of sight is closer to in-the-body physical sight than the other types. With this type of sight, objects seen while out of the body may look just like they do while in the body. This is the most desirable type of sight because it is easier for the physical brain to interpret the images seen during the OBE. The sight is focused at the astral body's eyes, and objects usually appear solid. Usually I have to make a special effort to employ this type of sight, and I've noticed that my peripheral vision isn't very good. Here is an example from my journals:

01/25/81 Sun—OBE #31

. . . Now I was fully conscious. I remembered my sight problem and decided to look at my waving arm, not sure if it was physical or astral. I looked over, and I saw my arm waving. It seemed to be physical sight. I felt sure I was in my physical body, trying to push myself out. Then I blacked out and woke up in my physical body and found out I had been wrong. I hadn't been in my physical body when I thought I was. My physical arm was wedged between my legs, so the arm I had seen waving was my astral arm. I had been seeing the astral counterpart of the physical world.

The following example illustrates another important point: eyesight (among other things) is affected by our beliefs and our thoughts.

02/23/80—OBE #9

. . . I looked up about thirty degrees and I didn't see my bookshelf, etc.; I saw a gray area, almost as if it were a time tunnel, like the old television show. But it was like a gray cloud. . . . The strangest thing I find about the astral plane is how astral sight works. It's like a truer "tunnel vision." You see only where you look, and then only what you expect or want to see. I didn't see any of the surroundings of my physical room. For example, I didn't see my dressers or bookshelf, but I could see my own astral body when I expected to see it. OBE #5 also involved the strange sense of sight. During that experience I saw the physical pillow, hand, etc., but not my astral hands. When I wanted to see what they were doing, I looked out in front, and slowly the *vision* of them swaying gently back and forth *faded in*. They slowly got clearer until I could recognize that they were my hands.

Astral Mind Sensing

Astral mind sensing is the type of eyesight that I've experienced most often during my OBEs. This isn't much like true eyesight at all. You can't actually "see" things, but you can "feel" with your mind where everything is. This type of sight isn't centered around astral eyes. Objects are "felt" in all directions simultaneously by the whole focus of consciousness. This type of sight is very hard to interpret or describe in physical terms. You can flawlessly navigate a cluttered room but not "see" any particular object in the room. Here are a few examples.

08/15/80—OBE #21

Sometime during the night I woke up in my astral body, gently swaying inside the physical body. I swayed myself and was mildly surprised when my consciousness swayed too. So I swayed myself harder until my astral feet touched the ground. . . . I decided to try to wake up my mother. So I struggled against the pull of my cord and walked through my door. I went down the kitchen hall and into my parents' bedroom. I saw both of their bodies sleeping there. My dad's body was talking in his sleep. I looked again to see if their bodies glowed from their auras. I didn't notice any glow. I decided to wake my mother up. So I reached out and tried to rouse her by shaking her while saying, "Wake up, Ma." She finally woke up and looked but didn't see me. I tried to get her attention, but she finally got up and walked through me!

Again, my vision had been funny; I had thought to look to see if I could see the glow of their auras and had made a special effort to "look" at their bodies. I couldn't really see, but I could sense things with my mind, sort of like radar. I could feel the presences of things always, but had to make a special effort to "see" with eyes. I realized that at the time, and I made a special effort to "look" so I could bring back a clear memory when I came back; the mind vision must be very hard to translate into physical terms by the brain.

Body Sight

Body sight is very annoying. I never read about it happening, nor did I think it was possible until I experienced it. This happens when you try to open your astral eyes and your physical eyes open instead, giving you a completely different and confusing perspective. With this type of sight, you can only see in the direction that the body's eyes are pointing. It is often out of focus. It resembles split-consciousness, except that your consciousness is still fully within the astral body. Here are a few examples from my journals.

11/29/80 Sat—OBE #27

. . . I was out of my body, floating about four feet away from it. I realized at once that I couldn't see, so I made an effort to open my eyes. At that exact moment, for a split second I had dual consciousness! I felt my physical body had opened its eyes, while at the same time I was floating above the body, looking down! In other words, I was plainly in my astral body, and I was looking down, but what I saw was from my physical body looking up! I got really confused, was shocked, surprised, whatever, and then I lost consciousness and started dreaming.

12/17/80 Wed—OBE #29

. . . I was falling asleep when I noticed that I had two sets of arms! I had a lot of control, but my consciousness was not too good. I forced myself down under my bed. I couldn't see anything, nor was I "mind sensing." But I could feel my [astral] body fine, and I knew where I was. I immediately drew myself up to the ceiling. I didn't propel myself up there, nor did I exactly "think" myself up there. I just drew myself up to the ceiling in what seemed like a natural manner. I still couldn't see. I tried to open my eyes, but it once again seemed as if my physical eyes opened, and I saw from my body's viewpoint. I recognized the danger of this (I might have gotten confused as I did in OBE #27). So I closed my eyes again.

01/24/81 Sat—OBE #30

. . . I was . . . about three inches below my physical body. I opened my eyes, and, although my astral self was swaying, my vision was not! I noticed that my sight was normal, and not the usual distorted astral vision, and I wondered why. Then it came to me. Once again, I was seeing through my physical eyes! This has happened before, but now I decided to investigate the matter further. It didn't make sense that I was seeing through my physical body's eyes. I decided to try to figure it out. I reached out my (astral) hand in front of me and my face. I looked through my physical eyes and saw nothing but the ceiling and the overhead light. My physical body wasn't seeing my astral arm, which I plainly felt as being right in front of my physical eyes. I didn't feel any discomfort, but I thought my physical eyes had been open a long time, and they needed blinking. So I blinked them, and it was a normal blink. I did it again. When I blinked, for that split second, it seemed as though my astral head floated up to meet my physical head. Then when I blinked I felt my head as being physical, although my astral legs were still dangling. Well, I decided that it would remain a mystery. I decided to go do something, so I pulled myself up about five feet above my body. I also closed my eyes so they wouldn't disturb me.

Clairvoyance

"Clairvoyance" is the term I use to define a whole grab bag of different types of sight, such as seeing auras and receiving images of people and places that aren't present. I believe that "remote viewing" mainly uses this type of sight, which used to be called "traveling clairvoyance" years ago. I believe anyone can learn to use this type of sight, whether out of the body or in, with practice. Here are a few examples from my OBE journals.

10/24/81 Sat—OBE #52

. . . I was off to another excursion. When I got out, I was about one foot above my body. I sat up. I knew what I must do. I had to get to LD's house somehow. I thought to myself, "I know there are two possible routes I could take, either the back door or out through my window." But I heard the back door open and shut. I directed my attention over there, and my clairvoyant vision opened up. I saw that it was my mom coming in from outside. I also noticed the clock in the kitchen, but it was too blurry to see the time. I remember that it was more like second sight or clairvoyant vision. . . .

05/15/82 Sat—OBE #73

. . . I looked down at my swaying legs, but all I saw was my bed. I saw no legs. I thought, "Well, now is the best time to practice clairvoyant vision because I know what to look for [my legs]." So I half-closed my astral eyes and put them out of focus. I experimented with my eyes, and finally after about six tries, I found how to hold my eyes so that they would get the clearest clairvoyant sight [of my legs]. I cannot possibly describe any more how I used my eyes to see that way; it is something that can only be gained through experimenting. Anyway, I was seeing clairvoyantly, and I clearly saw two identical sets of legs. One set (the physical) was resting on the bed. The other set (the astral) was swaying up and down, and the physical bed wasn't affecting it in the least. I feel now that I was actually using clairvoyant sight or "second sight" because I noticed a difference between it and the usual astral sight. The astral sight I am used to usually doesn't give me great detail. In this projection I saw my legs, the pajamas I was wearing, and the exact design on those pajamas. Ordinarily when I look at my legs astrally, I either see them as bare legs, or I see clothing vaguely. In this mode of vision I also noticed many other details. The neatest thing was being able to see both sets of legs there. Both sets of legs looked semi-transparent, and I could distinguish color very well.

07/25/82 Sun—OBE #80

. . . I looked at my astral arms, not astrally, but clairvoyantly, as if trying to see a spirit from the physical world. My astral arms looked like transparent, dark black, filmy shadows. I studied them for awhile, then blacked out.

Peculiarities of Sight

Astral travelers have always reported differences between the physical world and the OBE world. For instance, a door that is closed physically might appear open while out of the body. Why are there differences? The most common explanation is that we aren't really seeing the physical world: We are seeing the astral counterpart of the physical world. It is said that the astral world is very plastic and when left alone, it molds itself to the shape of physical objects. I've also seen some peculiar things while out of the body.

Seeing the Physical Body

What is it we're seeing while we're out of the body? If we're seeing only the astral counterpart of physical objects, it follows that we should not be able to see our own body. After all, we are already using the astral body. I haven't looked at my physical body much during OBEs, but when I do, it usually looks like a blob of gray. However, it hasn't always appeared as I expect:

04/27/80—OBE #15

Sometime this morning I found myself conscious out of my body, but very near it. My first instincts were to get away from it. So when I thought about getting away, I drifted down through my bed underneath my body. I could feel the bed as I went through it. I saw my body through the bed as a body-shaped mass of gray matter. I thought, "No, I don't want to go down. I want to go up." Then I drifted up above my body to the ceiling. I started to drift through the ceiling, and I could feel the layers go through my arms and head. It was so strange!

When I was halfway through the ceiling, I was sensing things with my mind and not using my astral sense of sight. I thought, "I'm supposed to see what's up here (above my room)." So I quickly turned my head to look, saw some stuff like a dresser flash by my sight, and the next thing I knew I was back in my body.

01/31/81 Sat—OBE #33

. . . I could see okay on the astral plane. I was in the high-vibration state, swaying. I was also about five inches below my physical body. My physical body from the astral plane looked like a ghost might appear on the physical plane. It looked to me to be a transparent shell in the shape of a man, with nothing in the middle.

01-15-84 Sun—OBE #101

. . . At that time I realized that my eyes were closed and I really wasn't seeing anything at all. My vision was totally dark. So I opened my astral eyes and turned around to look back at my body. The room looked normal. I could see everything in it. I looked at my bed, and it looked just like it should: all messed up. But there wasn't a body on it that I could see! I tried squinting, but I still didn't see my body. I did notice that the bed linen was flattened, as if there was some object on it, but the object was totally and completely invisible. I thought, "Oh that's interesting. I wonder why I can't see it." I closed my eyes and tried to turn on clairvoyance. I could barely mind-sense my body as a filmy, gray shadow on the bed. I just thought, "Hm. Oh well," and decided to go do something. . . .

Astral Clouds

During several experiences I noticed clouds of gray hanging in midair. I still don't know what they are or why they exist. They seem to be undefined astral matter.

Astral Lights

During a few OBEs I noticed a strange light that I could not explain. As far as I know, this is not common in OBEs, but many people have reported seeing similar lights during near death experiences (NDEs). Here are some examples from my journals.

12/20/79 Thu—OBE #4

. . . strong vibrations came. I stayed calm. They "took over." I came out of my body about four feet away. I saw a bright light to the west. I was halfway through my wall between my bedroom and the living room. I looked back and saw my body. I was then slowly drawn toward it. I thought, "No! I'm not done! I want to go to JP's house! I want to go to JP and CA! I want to go!" I was sucked partially into my body but kept part of me out. I could move both bodies (astral and physical). My arms were astral, but my eyes were both astral and physical! I waved my left arm right in front of my face and looked through my physical eyes. I couldn't see them! I could feel them there, but I couldn't see them. I wanted to see them, so suddenly I did. I could partially move my other limbs. I decided to go back and end the experience.

03/07/82 Sun—OBE #66

. . . I looked and I saw a tiny, but concentrated, pinpoint of bright light to the west, and up a little bit. I was intrigued by it and stared at it. It didn't seem to be a physical light. I tried focusing my eyes in a number of different ways to try to see it more clearly. I tried to look at it with physical sight, astral sight, mind sensing, and many other forms of sight. I tried to magnify it in my vision. I don't know why I was so fascinated with it. I started staring at it almost hypnotically. I wondered if it had anything to do with my body or if I was waking up. Then I felt my consciousness slowly transported back to my physical body, and I was still quite loose from my body. I started swaying again, but I felt all of my senses come slowly back to my body. The swaying became slower and slower, then finally stopped, and I came to.

Miscellaneous

Sometimes I've seen things that didn't make any sense.

06/27/82 Sun—OBE #76

. . . My eyes opened and I astrally saw a very blurry sight that did not make sense. This lasted for a split second, and it was followed by another picture that was very clear, but it was very short in duration. This second sight (vision) looked like a square rainbow or a square representation of the spectrum of light. I could see nothing but gray around this box of colors. In this box, leftmost, was a bigger block of pure black. To the right of the black portion were six or so other colors that were either in the order of the rainbow (red-orange-yellow-green-blue-violet) or in reverse order (violet-blue-green-yellow-orange-red). I remember it clearly. This box of colors was to the right [side] of my field of vision. Anyway, this vision faded, and I again saw the blurry first vision. Then I felt a tremendous electrical shock hit my system, as if I had stuck my finger into a light socket and received a full 110-volt electrical shock. This shock hit every cell of my body, and I was slammed back to my body. My heart was beating wildly, beyond control, as if the shock was physical.

Through practice, it is possible to learn to control out-of-body vision. I recommend you experiment with the different types of sight to see what works best for you. I recommend using a form of sight that can be expressed in physical terms when you return to your body and want to record the experience.

Objectivity of Sight

Many books on out-of-body experiences claim that OBEs are completely controlled by our thoughts, beliefs, expectations, and wishes. But if this is true, how "real" are these experiences? Where do they fit in with our experience of the "real" or "objective" world? If you leave your body and travel to Jupiter, and believe the planet is blue instead of orange, will you see a blue Jupiter or an orange one? In either case, are you really seeing the "real" planet, or one that was created in your mind? This is a very perplexing question that deserves more attention.

There are many people who have reported OBEs in which they saw things that really did happen. The most common of these are the descriptions by patients undergoing surgery, who claim to have witnessed the whole procedure from outside their body. Some have reported details of the procedure that they could not have possibly known, such as where the doctors put gall stones that were removed. Some patients have accurately repeated conversations that went on during the surgery. Skeptics may dismiss such cases by theorizing that some subconscious part of the patient still had cognitive abilities during the operation, and assuming that somehow the patient accessed this subconscious memory when they awoke. This theory cannot explain the less common cases where OBE subjects have reported what was happening in a different room. These seem to suggest that the subject could actually see some part of physical reality.

There are also many cases where people saw things during an OBE that didn't correspond to the physical world. For instance, take the following OBE:

12/21/85 Sat—OBE #119

I brought myself down into the proper mental state very easily, and I got out of my body using an older technique: I waited for a certain feeling in the pit of my stomach, moved my consciousness down to my abdomen, then lifted myself straight up at that place, and out of the body. It all happened very quickly, and it seemed ridiculously easy at the time.

I was in midair floating about two feet above my physical body. I turned to my left (south), and raised myself into a standing position. I looked at the north wall and briefly considered whether to walk through it. I decided against it.

I took a few steps toward the back of the bedroom, to the west. I felt a bit giddy and off balance. Then I took a few steps east, toward the bedroom door again. I felt unsure of my footing, and I assumed it was because I was too close to my physical body. I decided that I had to get farther away from my body, and the safest way to do that was to crawl on my hands and knees.

I got down on my hands and knees, and crawled toward the bedroom door, crawled through the bedroom door, and out into the living room. I crawled about six feet more until I was in the middle of the living room, and then stood up again and walked over toward the kitchen.

I looked into the kitchen, and it looked different. At the time I was standing partially through the microwave oven stand, but I didn't notice it or any of the other nearby objects in the room. I looked toward the countertop right of the sink, and there was no countertop! It appeared as if someone had cut out the countertop at the sink, all the way back to the wall, and the wall looked somewhat dirty. It looked as if whoever cut the countertop out had done a very sloppy job. I scanned the area up and down, and finally I said to myself, "It's an illusion; I know the kitchen isn't like this, but that's not important."

I walked back into the living room, stopped by JH's computer, and suddenly I became very excited. I said aloud (or so it seemed), "This is great! I'm completely lucid! This is entirely real!" I examined my own consciousness, and it was very clear, bright, lucid, and normal in every respect.

Why are there discrepancies between the physical and nonphysical worlds? Some people claim that astral matter is easily malleable and imitates physical objects, but not completely. Others claim it's because some OBEs occur in the "astral plane," which is influenced by our beliefs and expectations. Or perhaps the people who find themselves in a thought-influenced, subjective OBE state are really having lucid dreams.

Another theory is that some people have a kind of "clairvoyance" that allows them to see the physical world during an OBE, much as a clairvoyant can see spirits while in the body. Again, more research is needed to answer these questions.

EXERCISE 18
Rocking Chair Visualization

This is a variation of the previous exercise.

Before you attempt the exercise, sit in a rocking chair, close your eyes, and rock. Memorize the feeling of rocking with your eyes closed. This is how you should feel when you are doing the exercise.

You can do this either lying down or sitting. First, close your eyes and relax. As vividly as you can, imagine that you're sitting in a rocking chair, rocking gently forward and backward. Take your time doing this. In this exercise, it's not important to visualize at all. As a matter of fact, you can completely ignore any visual images that come to mind. In previous exercises, I wanted you to vividly pretend you were seeing images, like the yo-yo exercise in chapter 9. This time, I want you to vividly imagine the *feeling* of rocking back and forth. Keep at it until it seems as if your consciousness is *really* rocking.

Once again, this is more than just a silly exercise. I've used this imaginary feeling of rocking to leave my body. Actually, I used a slight variation, which went as follows. Some good movie theaters have seats like rocking chairs, but they have very tight springs. The tight springs make them more "springy" than regular rocking chairs, and they rock very quickly. Anyway, I would imagine I was sitting in one of these springy theater seats and start rocking. Pretty soon the vibrations would come, and I'd use the momentum to catapult away from the body.

Again, this exercise is very important. For me, it's probably one of the more effective exercises because it deals directly with feelings and bodily sensations instead of visualizations or imaginary sounds.

19

The Mind During OBEs

Some researchers have theorized that the problems encountered in visual experiments are not problems with vision, but rather problems with the mind and its interpretation of those images. Obviously, we can learn a lot about our reality and ourselves if we examine our own minds and consciousness during OBEs.

Consciousness

How is out-of-body consciousness different from normal consciousness? My experiments have led me to believe that out-of-body consciousness is very focused and directed. This single-mindedness makes it easier to induce the experience and usually stays with me during the experience. This focus also makes it easier to remember details of an experience. It can also be a hindrance, because it's tempting to divert your full attention to some small distraction during the experience, rather than doing something that you had planned. For instance, several times I induced an OBE with the hope to astrally visit a friend, but often I would become distracted and forget my goal.

I have experienced many frames of mind and states of consciousness during OBEs. Usually my consciousness is

completely normal in all respects. At times my consciousness is very strong, and I feel more awake and aware than
in normal life. But sometimes my consciousness feels very
weak. I've often used the analogy between consciousness
and a light bulb that is on a dimmer switch. In chapter
10, OBE #52 gave a fairly good idea of how consciousness
operates during an OBE. Here are some more examples.

05/23/82 Sun—OBE #74

. . . Then something happened that might be difficult to
describe. It seems as if my consciousness dimmed to the
point where I couldn't organize memories. The memory I
have is of time standing still. I remember tiny flashbacks
of things happening, but they all seemed to have happened at once. I remember seeing DB, and I remember
him walking back and forth. He came toward me, then
walked through me. Later, he opened the cabin door, and
the door went partway through my astral body. I also feel I
had some interaction with JP and CA. But my consciousness was so dim that I didn't have conscious control, and
my memory is so jumbled about that part that I can't say
any more [for certain].

05/02/83 Mon—OBE #94

. . . I went to bed around 10:00 P.M. I tried to project for
a little while, but I was just too mentally tired. I gave up
and rolled over onto my right side to go to sleep, but I
kept thinking about projection. I fell asleep almost immediately. The next thing I knew I was semiconscious and
out of my body, in my bedroom. I was standing up when
I noticed my condition. I examined my consciousness to
see how wide awake I really was; I wanted to make sure
I wasn't dreaming or deceiving myself in any other way.

I came to the conclusion that I was fully conscious in all respects. With that thought, my consciousness brightened suddenly until I was more conscious and aware than I am in waking life. I felt wonderful, alive, and vibrant, radiating with life and consciousness. I thought, "Wow! Now this is consciousness, better and more real than I've felt before!" And I felt completely free from my body. I could tell it was very dark there in my bedroom, but my eyesight was more astral than physical. I didn't hesitate to jump forward—through physical objects—to attempt flight. I closed my eyes and flew forward through my house, passing through walls and other physical objects as I gained speed. I felt each physical object as I passed through it, yet it didn't disturb me. I traveled so fast that I was out of the house in a few quick seconds. Once outside, I flew up and up, but I blacked out before I had a chance to do anything, or see where I was.

Logical Thinking

One of the things I try to examine during my OBEs is how "normal" my thoughts are. In most of my OBEs I seem to have normal, logical thoughts. Here are some examples.

08/02/81 Sun—OBE #45

. . . I woke up once at about 3:30 A.M. or 4:00 A.M. and went back to sleep. I dreamed that I was in a store at the university when I was called to a special counter. I received a phone call to come home immediately because of a death in the family. I asked the woman, "Who has died?" She said she couldn't tell me. All she could tell me was the person's Social Security number. I talked to the woman a long time and finally reasoned that it was my father (he's still alive). I was shocked and terribly sad. I decided to quit the dream.

So I tried to wake up, opened my eyes, and saw unfamiliar surroundings. I was stiff and felt paralyzed. My vision was weird too. I decided that I wasn't seeing truthfully. I didn't realize that I was astral; a bit of grogginess still hindered my thoughts. So I tried to remember where I should be and what I should be seeing. I decided I should be in bed looking up and seeing my walls with posters and the ceiling. My vision blurred away. When it returned, I saw my posters and all, but there was a strange piece of woodwork that doesn't exist in my room. "This isn't quite right either!" I reasoned that I could probably project easily. (I still didn't know I was nonphysical.)

Then I thought of the dream. If my father had just died, I wouldn't want to project. I'd be afraid. At the thought of projecting, I started to sway away from my body. But I pulled myself back because I wanted to think this situation through fully before I dared to leave my body's vicinity.

I reasoned further: "This prospect of Dad being dead was only in a dream. Yet, if he is dead, it is very possible that I would be informed of it in a dream. And if so, he may take the form of a ghost or leave a nasty astral shell about." I started to pull away from my body again on my own. I pulled myself back. I decided not to try to project further, just in case. I lost consciousness and woke up in my body after a few seconds of what seemed like nonexistence. I opened my eyes and saw how my room really looks and felt my body again. Then I changed my mind, but it was already too late. I noticed my entranced state of mind, though, and tried to project again with one near success.

I gained at least one good thing from this experience, and that is the knowledge of the proper state of mind conducive to astral projection. I wonder what causes this state of mind and body, and plan to read some books on sleep and the causes and effects of certain types of sleep. I slept very deeply. My body was stiff, and I couldn't feel it until I moved it and stretched. My mind was almost entranced. I was in a staring mood and found concentrating very easy. It was very easy to focus my mind on one thought. It was semi-easy to visualize. I probably ruined my chance to project again when I moved my body and broke its stiffness.

11/08/81 Sun—OBE #55

. . . [During the experience] my consciousness was again very clear and concise, but I was still very sleepy. I thought about doing some experimenting. Then I decided to follow my original plan of action: walk out of my house normally but as fast as I could, and then try to fly to LD's house. I thought of some parts of a song, and then I realized it was typical in-the-body thinking and made a mental note to myself to remember that my thought patterns are the same there as they are on earth.

Here is another example of logical thinking during an OBE. Notice the use of logical deduction during this OBE.

06/09/82 Wed—OBE #75

. . . This morning at 6:00 A.M. I was dreaming happily. In one dream, I was outside my bedroom, and I looked in through the window. I saw something that frightened me and put me in a state of awe. I don't remember what I saw, but I also thought I saw a blinding white light shining through my window. It seemed to be alive. The brightness didn't hurt my eyes. The white rays of light coming into my bedroom were like beautiful little fingers reaching out. At the sight of this (in a dream still), I let myself fall backward until I was on my back. The falling was very gentle, and I landed softly, weightlessly. I floated there for a few seconds and the dream changed. I had a deep level of awareness that told me that the dreams were all very important lessons, and I must watch them all. I don't remember any of the dreams now. This dream of projecting happened in the middle of the series of dreams I had to witness.

When the dreams were through, a certain part of me expressed an interest in the projection part. I wanted to do that dream over. So I saw myself outside my room again. I turned and looked again. Then I saw the sight in the window again. I fell over backward once more. But this time, when I landed on my back, I woke up. I was still in a weird state of consciousness, but I wasn't exactly dreaming. I had conscious control, so I levitated myself until I was lying at a slant outside my bedroom. My body was rigid. I was looking west, and my torso was parallel to my bedroom. I thought about how easy it was to levitate. I also noticed that the state I was in seemed somehow different from normal projection. I thought, "Wow! This is neat! I wonder if it is really a projection; it feels so different." To test my theory, I bent my right arm and put my right hand in front of my face. My logic was this: if I could see through my hand, it was probably a normal projection, but if I couldn't see through it, it was probably different. I fully expected to be able to see through my hand. But when I reached my hand out in front of me, I could not see through it. It seemed (looked) solid. I thought,

"Boy, that's strange! What else could it be then? I suppose that really isn't a good test. I could still be projecting." Then I started thinking about something else. Then I was frightened half to death when I heard my alarm clock go off. I was violently pulled back inside my body, and I came to with a jolt. My heart was pounding wildly from the fright.

Emotions

Are emotions any different while out of the body? Usually my emotions are normal during OBEs. Even my sense of humor isn't lost during my OBEs. However, I had the following experience during which I was very emotional. I even became hysterical, for no apparent reason:

01/30/82 Sat—OBE #62

Last night I stayed up until 12:30 A.M. watching a late movie, and then did some stretching until 1:00 or 1:30 A.M. I woke up early this morning and went back to sleep. After a while I seemed to feel a tingling sensation, and I came to full consciousness. I knew I was about to project, and I was aware of the vibrations at a certain level of consciousness. So I made a quick movement, and I sat up (astrally) wondering what I should do. Then I suddenly was overcome with thoughts of my father who had physically died 17 days ago. I cried, "Daddy!" hoping to see him on the astral plane. I was about two feet above my body, and I was mostly not seeing but mind sensing. I relaxed to a semi-reclined position in midair. I looked up in the corner of my bedroom where I thought I had seen some movements. I was very emotional for some reason, and it was almost a panic state. I became hysterical soon, and I reached my arms out in front of me, hoping that my father or someone would take my hands and help me away from my body. But I couldn't stand it. It was less than one second of time later that I became completely hysterical and *screamed*, *"Daddy!"* as loudly as I possibly could, and with as much emotion as I have ever known in my life.

The last thing I remember was that I looked hopelessly into the astral fog. Then I blacked out very completely and very deeply. The next thing I knew I was dreaming, two or more hours later. I have absolutely no memory of what happened between the time I blacked out and when I started dreaming.

It completely baffles me as to why I was so emotional, so hysterical during this experience. And I was impatient. Usually when I project, I stay calm. But this time was just the opposite. I just don't understand. All I can do is to explain my actual emotions during the experience. I somehow wanted frantically for him to come to me, take my hands, help me away from my body, cradle me, and make me his child. I somehow couldn't wait, even a few seconds, for my dad to arrive. My final shriek was a frantic plea to him, to my guides, or to anyone to come and just be with me in a world where they are tangible and real and can be hugged—a place where they have solidity.

I really don't understand it. I feel completely different now, but those were my feelings at the time.

In comparison, the following OBE happened about a month later, in which I met and talked with my deceased father. This time I was completely calm, rational, and logical during the experience.

03/02/82 Tue—OBE #65

. . . I astrally projected last night and talked to my dad who died less than two months ago. I had been flying and woke up out of my body as I landed. My dad was coming into view, and I landed next to him. I couldn't see anything but him: there wasn't anything around for miles except blackness. He had a T-shirt on, and he looked very good. Here's what we said:

Bob: Dad!

Dad: Hi, Bob. You guys are a little preoccupied with my death, aren't you?

Bob: Yeah, I guess so. What should I tell them?

Dad: Tell 'em I love them. Tell Mom she shouldn't be so sad. It had to be this way.

Bob: What about the direction of my life?

Dad: Don't worry. Everything will turn out all right.

We exchanged one more line (which I don't remember). Then I remember (vaguely) flying for many miles downward and over until I was next to my body. I woke up right away. I thought about it for awhile, but I was overcome by sleep. I have dreamed about him before, and this was not a dream. First, there is always scenery in a dream, and there wasn't any there. Second, in a dream I am watching myself do things against my conscious will. But there I was conscious. I didn't see myself because I *was* myself. And everything I did was my own conscious choice.

The only thing I noticed about this projection was that I was strangely intellectual. I wasn't emotional but had the feeling of a thinking mind. I didn't think to ask him any of a million questions I'd like to ask him. The lack of scenery makes me believe this incident took place on the astral plane, if there is such a place.

Right Brain/Left Brain

During an out-of-body experience, is there some separation between the right and left hemispheres of the brain? Which part of the brain interprets nonphysical experiences? Scientists have shown that one side of the brain (usually the left side) is more logical and mathematical, and tends to put labels on the objects it sees. The other side of the brain is mainly used for aesthetics, emotions, and things of an artistic nature. If the OBE was strictly devoted to the right hemisphere, it would explain why Ingo Swann could see and draw the American flag "target," but did not label it as a flag. It would also explain some difficulty people have identifying targets in OBE experiments.

The following OBE seems to suggest that OBEs are, to some degree, interpreted by the right hemisphere of the brain, but we have the power to control our brain during the experience:

04/13/85 Sat—OBE #112

I went to bed at 2:00 A.M. and was awakened by the telephone at 8:00 A.M. When I went back to bed, I decided to try to have an OBE. I practiced until I felt tired, then I rolled over and decided to try going to sleep with OBE on my mind. I fell asleep. I woke up a few times, rolled over, and went to sleep thinking about OBE again.

Then at about 10:50 A.M. I became conscious, but I felt strange, and I thought I might be out of my body. I became fully conscious and decided I was out of my body.

I lifted myself slowly into the air about two feet with my mind. I didn't notice anything in my bedroom because my eyesight was strange, but when I was about three feet away from my body, I noticed an object. The object was off in the distance and hanging in midair.

I didn't recognize the object right away, but it was shaped almost like a human head: it was white, and it had dark prongs on top, as though the head were wearing a crown. I thought, "I can go anywhere I want now . . . but if I don't find out what that object is, it will bother me the rest of my life," I stopped my forward motion and floated weightlessly in the air. 1 turned toward the white object and looked at it. It appeared filmy and transparent.

At first I thought it was a materialized head with a crown, all made of ectoplasm, similar to the objects and faces seen in "spirit photography." I focused on it more and started to notice certain details: the "chin" area was square. I became very determined to solve the mystery of what it was, regardless of whether or not it was dangerous. I mentally pulled myself toward the object and tried to focus on it more.

I figured I was seeing it with my emotions, as if I were using the right side of my brain. So I tried to engage my intellect, or the left side of my brain [by solving mathematical problems in my mind]. As I did this, the object became clear—it was my nearest aloe vera plant, sticking out of its white pot. As it came into focus, the rest of the room also came into focus, and I could see everything in my bedroom clearly.

I decided to get up and walk out of my bedroom. I started to upright myself and headed toward the door. Then my consciousness became dim, and I was pulled into my body and came to.

The aloe plant, sitting in its white vase, was an everyday object in my bedroom. In waking life, I could have recognized it in an instant. However, at the beginning of the OBE, I could tell its size, shape, and color, and yet was unable to "recognize" it or see its texture. It seemed almost two-dimensional and without depth. I should also mention that there were two other aloe plants, in dark brown vases, sitting next to the plant in the white vase. The three plants were sitting in a row on top of my dresser. Until my vision became clear, I only saw the one plant, and it looked as if it was hanging in midair.

When I tried to purposely engage the left side of my brain by solving mathematical problems, the other objects in the room came into focus, and I recognized the plant for what it was.

At face value, it seems that out-of-body experiences are profoundly affected by our use of the right and left hemispheres of the brain. Our OBEs may be valuable on a soul or spirit level, but if our physical brain is unable to interpret the experiences in its own terms, we might not return to our bodies with much of value. And we might not be able to describe the experiences to others. This right brain/left brain idea is very intriguing, and I feel it needs more investigation. This may lead us to discover why our brains are divided into parts.

EXERCISE 19
Workout and Visualized Books

Here is an exercise to help you focus your consciousness. I have noticed that my mind is less "muddy" after I have been exercising for about a half hour to an hour. Try exercising vigorously for about an hour in the middle of the day, and then make your OBE attempt.

There is a fine line between too much exercise and not enough. Too much exercise will make you too tired, and you'll drop off to sleep. Too little exercise, and you are likely to be too focused inside your body. Try different combinations to find out what works best for your metabolism.

Lie down after your workout, and visualize a book in front of you. Mentally open the book and try to visualize words on the pages. You can imagine the book any way you want with pictures and writing in various colors. Strive to make the printing look clear in your mind's eye so you can read the pages. Of course, the visualized book has nothing to do with OBEs; this exercise is merely to help you learn to focus your mind down to a single thread.

After holding this visualization for a while, you may be suddenly "zapped" into a state of intense awareness. Then the vibrations may sweep over you, separating you from your body.

20

The Fantasy Trap

In my attempts to explore the out-of-body state, I've discovered a psychological "trap" that can stop or delay an OBE. I call it the "fantasy trap," and it's caused by daydreaming in the OBE state. I can explain it best by giving an example from my journals.

11/29/81 Sun—OBE #58

... My consciousness was starting to get dim, so I wrestled with it for awhile and took hold of a clean, clear consciousness. I thought to myself how strange it was that my projection was lasting so long.

I wanted to get away so strongly that I started to use my mind to pretend to go to places. In essence, I started to fantasize. It was very much like the normal dream state.

In the first fantasy I walked out into the living room. JP, CA, Mom, and Dad were there, talking. I walked out and sat down. I said something like, "You can see me!", then they said, "Of course we can see you." Then I thought, "This can't be right; I'm projecting."

Just then I came out of it and came to realize I had been fantasizing. I was still stuck to my body in the same position.

I tried again to use my mind to get away and slipped into another fantasy. In this fantasy I walked up to my bedroom door, opened it and went through. I walked to the nearest window and tried to walk through it. But it seemed very solid. So I very quickly went to the back door, ignoring everything else. I opened the door and walked outside. I went to the nearest clearing and jumped up into the air in a Superman pose. Then I fell flat on my face! It seemed so very physical that I began to doubt I was projecting. I thought, "Well, now I've made a complete fool of myself. I must be physical." I started walking toward the house again, but I never got there. It was then I came to realize that I had been fantasizing again.

I was dumbfounded by my own wishful-thinking fantasy. Then I was fully conscious and compared the fantasies to my awakened state. I thought, "Well, that use of my mind will only lead me to self-deception. I should stick to getting away using my astral body." So I tried to pry my astral body free and managed to get unstuck for a while. I crawled over to my bedroom window and tried to press through it. I couldn't press through it; it seemed solid. Just then I blacked out and woke up in my physical body. I looked at the time and it was 10:20 A.M. My experience must have lasted fifteen or twenty minutes.

The fantasy trap can be quite persistent and annoying, as you can see from the following example.

04/16/83 Sat—OBE #93

. . . I quickly discovered that I was now stuck to the physical body, and I struggled to get free of it. I struggled for what seemed to be ten or fifteen minutes, using only my mind to try to free myself. After that I started thinking of other things and, because I was very tired, I eventually lapsed into a daydream, which led me into a state of hypnogogic imagery again. I was now semiconscious. At some level of consciousness, I was still aware of my OBE condition. It was only a minute or two before I "caught myself" and re-established full consciousness.

Once again I tried to unstick myself from the body. I tried several things. I tried to pull myself up to the ceiling and send my consciousness to the ceiling by imagining the point of view of looking down at my body. I got a brief "clairvoyant" image of my body down on the bed, but I didn't actually travel up there. I pondered the image for a while; my body looked rather beat. I wanted to float up and get a real look at it from my actual astral body's point of view. I tried for a while longer to get free, but once again I lapsed into semiconsciousness. After a long time of dream-like short scenes, I finally snapped out of it again, and I was still out of my body but stuck to it.

I thought, "I'm really out of my body!" Then I said, "Wow! I'm really projecting. I'm even speaking aloud while out of my body!" Then the humor of what I had just said and the fact that I was talking to myself caught up with me, and I chuckled aloud. I laughed a while longer, then set out to free myself again. This time I was sitting up, but was still stuck to the body by my lower half. I tried desperately to float myself up to the ceiling, but couldn't. Again, I started thinking hard about how to get free, but fell into semiconsciousness again. After several short scenes, I caught myself yet again.

I was still out of my body, and this time when I awoke out of it, I spent a few minutes "comparing" the two states of mind, the semiconscious (fantasy) state . . . and the pure waking, out-of-body state where I had full awareness of everything. I thought about the differences for awhile, and I finally resolved not to fall prey again to that delusive state of semiconscious OBE-mind. But after a few minutes, I fell back into it anyway.

I awoke again, still out of my body, and was surprised the experience was lasting so long; it seemed like at least an hour since the initial jump out of my body. I also noted how easy it was for me to fall into that semiconscious state, although I had made a firm resolution not to. So I perked up my consciousness, as I normally do to keep myself from sleeping (e.g., while driving). "What should I do now?" I thought (and I thought about it for several minutes) and finally fell prey to semiconsciousness yet again! This time I did not catch myself, but instead allowed my subconscious to take complete control.

I entered the physical body while still semiconscious and started to dream. I woke up in my physical body when the telephone rang, startling me considerably.

I took great notice of another phenomenon when I was first out of my body—my heartbeat. Throughout the experience of leaving the body, I paid special attention to my physical heartbeat. Just before I left the body, my heartbeat had slowed down considerably. It remained very slow until the vibrations hit me. With the coming of the vibrations and the "trauma" of leaving the body, my heartbeat sped up to a very rapid pace. It was as if I had just received a terrible fright and my heart was beating wildly from a "fight or flight" response. Once I was out of my body, I listened very carefully for my heartbeat. Although it had slowed down again, it was still much faster than my normal waking heart rate. After that, I didn't notice my heart rate; I was totally oblivious of my body.

Most of the OBE books say that you can travel in the blink of an eye, just by thinking about the person or place you want to visit. Therefore, I would think about a place I wanted to visit, and I would visualize that place and imagine I was there.

I learned this form of idle imagination can easily turn into an unproductive OBE-daydream. Instead of being transported, the visualization takes on a life of its own, and my consciousness slips into a dream-fantasy state. The fantasy is entirely subjective, as far as I can tell, and can be as wild as any ordinary dream. But once the fantasy is over and my consciousness returns to normal, I know I've been dreaming.

When I return to full consciousness, I may still be out of my body. Waking up out of body (and comparing the former dream to the now-OBE state) convinces me that the OBE was real (objective) and that the fantasy was not real (subjective).

If you fall prey to the fantasy trap, there are certain clues that you are no longer in the proper state: fantasy objects (such as doors and windows) might seem solid, fantasy people might see you, and your fantasy body might not be able to fly.

If you wake up in the body from a dream fantasy, you might be left with a sense of "Was that just a dream?" I usually say something like, "this is real!" during OBEs so that I'll have a conscious point of reference. Of course, I only say that after I examine my state of consciousness and detect that I am fully aware during the experience. That way, I leave no doubts that I was conscious at the time and not involved in a dream fantasy.

EXERCISE 20
Breathing

Many people claim that a key factor in inducing out-of-body experiences is breathing properly. Famous OBE researcher Robert Crookall devoted a book to the subject, called *Psychic Breathing*.

Breathing exercises have many benefits. Deep breathing will help you to relax your body for the OBE. Breathing exercises, if done correctly, can bring you energy that may prolong the experience. Also, it can improve your ability to focus. I recommend doing breathing exercises before you try to induce an OBE, and not during the induction.

Here are some pointers for your breathing exercises. Babies breathe naturally because they haven't learned our bad habits. If you've ever watched a baby breathe, you may notice its belly rises and falls, but its chest doesn't. Babies breathe using their abdomens, not by forcing their lungs to rise and fall. Try to do the same: breathe from your abdomen, not from your lungs.

During your breathing exercise, breathe in through your nose and out through your mouth. As you inhale, visualize that your lungs are being filled with white light. As you exhale, visualize that all your fears, worries, problems, and health problems are flowing out of your body.

Some people believe that visualizing a flow of energy can activate your chakras (energy centers), which can help you achieve OBEs. In some forms of Taoist meditation, people are taught to visualize a stream of energy flowing in a circle that starts near the navel, travels down to the groin, up the spine, over the head, down the chest and back to the navel. Kundalini yoga teaches a similar thing, but the energy doesn't flow in a circle, it flows out through the top of the head. I don't recommend the latter method because some Taoists claim that it's dangerous to push the energy out your head.

When you try to induce an OBE, just relax and let your breathing become normal again. Don't try to breathe differently in any way. It may be helpful, however, to quietly listen to the sound of your own breath.

During the OBE, it may suddenly seem as if you have stopped breathing. If this happens, don't be alarmed. Your body is still breathing, but you have lost awareness of the body.

21

People and Animals

People often ask me, do you ever meet anyone while you're out of your body? Yes., I have, but not often. In perhaps 10 percent of my OBEs, I have had interaction with other people. There are two categories of people you are likely to meet during an OBE: physical and nonphysical. A physical person is inside his or her physical body during your OBE. A nonphysical person can be someone who is also having an OBE, or a person who is without a physical body—"dead."

When you meet someone on the astral plane, it's easy to tell if they are physical or nonphysical. The physical people usually seem preoccupied with trivialities. If you meet up with a physical person, he or she will usually be busily preoccupied with reading, doing dishes, or another physical activity. They don't seem to notice you. You can speak with them, but usually they won't look at you while they speak, although sometimes it may seem as if they look at you. Physical people are always affected by gravity. Also, physical people usually have irregular or discolored auras.

On the other hand, nonphysical people are not preoccupied. They usually notice you, and look at you when they are talking. They often wear out-of-place clothes. And they can be found perched in midair or just about anywhere. Quite often in my experience, I've been able to hear or "feel" the presence of discarnates, but haven't been able to see them. Also, their auras are mostly clear, regularly shaped, and evenly colored.

There may also be cases where nonphysical people don't seem to notice you. A good example of this is OBE #116, mentioned in chapter 16, where I saw a group of people in my room, dressed in 1950s-style clothes. In these cases, I'm not sure if I am seeing spirits from a different "wavelength" or some sort of psychic after-image.

Physical People

In Robert Monroe's first book, he believed that when we are speaking to a physical person, we are talking with their subconscious minds. He described elaborate conversations with people while he was out of his body, but when he tried to verify the experience, nobody remembered the conversations. His theory seems to fit perfectly with my experiences. Talking to a physical person is strained, as if they are too preoccupied to talk with you. Or perhaps their conscious minds feel uneasy about having their subconscious talking with a "spirit." It seems as though physical people are so focused on their daily lives that they feel uncomfortable turning any portion of their consciousness away from that focus. For example, during OBE #21 mentioned in chapter 18, when I tried to rouse my mom from sleep, she just seemed to ignore me. Here are a few more examples from my journals.

05/02/81 Sat—OBE #39

. . . I walked through the living room of JP's apartment and entered JP and CA's bedroom. Both JP and CA were in bed. CA was laying down with her eyes closed. JP was sitting up in bed with some reading material. I jumped up and down and waved my hands to try to get JP's attention. He looked up at me. Then he nudged CA and she stirred. He pointed at me and said, "Look. I think there's something there." She looked, but didn't say anything. I didn't want them to be afraid of me, so I said, "It's me, Bob. I'm projecting." JP then said, "It's probably Bob projecting," as though he didn't hear me. He went back to reading. I said, "How can I be sure I'm going to remember this? What if I forget? I've got to remember." JP said, "Don't worry, we'll remember for you." I said, "How can I be sure you will remember?" He said, "We're awake. We should remember." I said, "Okay, but I may still forget." He said, "Don't worry about it; you'll remember."

When I asked JP and CA about this incident later that day, they didn't remember anything. JP was reading at the time. CA was awake but doing various things around the apartment. But several times, she had reclined on the bed to relax for a few minutes. Here's another example.

07/30/81 Thu—OBE #44

. . . Well, I turned around and saw my father sitting in a kitchen chair with a sad expression on his face. I didn't want to speak, but I tried to get his attention by waving my hands in the place he seemed to be staring, I was about six or seven feet away from him. He finally looked up and said something like, "Oh. Hello." I said, "Hi!

Look! I'm projecting!" With that, I decided to continue on, not wanting to waste any projecting time, and Dad didn't seem interested.

Nonphysical People

The experience quoted above happened when my father was alive. The following experience happened after his death:

12/20/81 Sun—OBE #60

. . . I twisted and reached for the window. I tried to pull myself toward it with my mind. My consciousness was dimmed again, but this time I thought I saw a small boy of twelve or so (years old) watching me from the northeast upper corner of my bedroom (by my window). I felt two or three older people that were on the other side of my bedroom wall. The boy said something to me, and then he talked with the older people for awhile. I don't remember what was said. The boy had dark brown hair, sparkling eyes, and a grin that seemed to indicate that he was pleased and mischievous because I was out of my body. . . . The older people were standing up. One was male, one female, and I didn't see the third well. These older people appeared to be about thirty-five to forty years old and were more serious than the boy. I became aware of these older people only when they spoke to the boy and he answered. Just as I lost consciousness, I saw the boy slide down what appeared to be a ladder.

In this OBE, several people seemed to be watching me and speculating about me. They seemed to know me, as if they were my spirit guides, but I didn't consciously know any of them. The grinning boy seemed as if he was pleased with me. He acted lively and mischievous, with his big grin and sparkling eyes. However, none of them seemed to want to communicate with me. It was as if they were scientists during an experiment, and I was the subject.

Animals

Some animals have more powerful senses than people. Dogs and cats can often see flying insects that our eyes miss unless we look closely. Animals also seem to be naturally psychic. I've talked to many people who have said their pets exhibited unusual behavior, such as staring off into space or circling their heads as if they were seeing spirits. Those people have looked for insects and other possible "normal" explanations for such behavior without success. My family never had a pet by the time I was experiencing OBEs, but JP had a cat named Zack. During one OBE, I encountered Zack in JP's apartment. It was my only encounter with an animal during an out-of-body experience.

10/21/83 Fri—OBE #98

This happened on 10/18/83: I've only had a chance to write it down now. I was having strange dreams and became semiconscious. Then I noticed I was weightless, and that realization brought me to a fuller consciousness: I woke up. I was in JP's living room and I saw JP's cat Zack, and he seemed to see me. I decided that, as long as I was a spirit, and I was near Zack, I should try to frighten him to prove to myself that he saw me. So I stood up tall, raised my arms, and started to run, reaching toward Zack. That cat ran very quickly away!

EXERCISE 21
A Ship's Bow

This exercise is similar to the theater chair method. Relax completely. As vividly as you can, imagine you are standing on the bow (front) of a ship in the middle of the ocean. Imagine the water is completely calm, and you are looking out over the water. You are completely at peace. Slowly, waves start to kick up and the boat starts to rock up and down. As the boat rocks up, feel yourself lift up. As the boat rocks down, feel yourself gently set down again. Gradually, make each wave bigger until the waves are ten feet high. With each wave, you rise and fall rhythmically. As you fall with each new wave, try to feel that sinking sensation in the pit of your stomach as if you are really there.

Again, this can call the vibrations and pull you away from your body.

Out of Body Experiences

22

Out-of-Body Reality

M any books about out-of-body experiences say that
during an OBE, our thoughts produce instant reality. Well, maybe not instantly. Sometimes it seems as if
our subconscious thoughts are more powerful than our
conscious thoughts. Our beliefs, expectations, and fears
also play a large part in what we experience while out of
our bodies.

For instance, why do you even have an astral body?
While you are out of your body, why should you need a
body at all? Why do you need astral hands? If you try to
pick something up, your hands will pass right through the
object. Why do you need astral eyes? With mind sensing, you can sense everything around you without even
using your eyes. Why do you need astral legs if you can
just as easily float or fly wherever you want? The answer
is, you don't need an astral body! We have astral bodies
because we are so accustomed to operating with a body,
and it's part of our self-image. We believe in our bodies so
strongly that we create astral bodies for ourselves to use
during an OBE. Perhaps we also do it as a convenience
to others. How would we recognize a friend if he or she
didn't have an astral body with their familiar face?

Let's take this one step further. During an OBE, are we naked or do we wear clothes? The answer is, sometimes we are naked, but most of the time we do wear astral clothes. The few people who report being naked during an OBE usually "feel naked" without their body.

Others report that they were wearing white robes, unlike any clothes they own in physical life. These people usually believe that they are dead or they are temporarily spirits—and what else do spirits wear?

There are also many people who find themselves in astral clothes identical to the clothes they were wearing at the time of the OBE. Often these people don't realize at first that they are out of their bodies. One moment they lie down for a nap, and the next moment they find themselves standing up and feeling light on their feet. And of course, they believe they are wearing the same clothes.

More common, however, is the case where the subject doesn't remember whether he or she was wearing clothes. They just don't seem to notice. That is usually the case during my OBEs. I don't think about the clothes I am wearing, and since I'm not thinking about it, no clothes are created. And I don't even notice the clothes are missing.

The point is, while we are out of the body, our beliefs do influence our experience. Our thoughts also influence our experience, but they are subject to our beliefs.

Not only does this law work for astral objects like clothes, but for our astral bodies as well. If we believe our astral bodies are malleable, they will be. Some people have reported their astral bodies were not in the shape of a human body, but in another shape. Take the following OBE for example:

Out of Body Experiences

11/08/81 Sun—OBE #55

. . . I separated my head last, and then I felt just like a balloon. I was bouncing up and down but stuck to my body in a way I could not tell. I couldn't turn around. My consciousness was again very clear and concise. . . . If I had an astral body, then it was curled up into a ball-shape. And I was stuck to my body's right side; that is, by the right arm.

After experiencing a few OBEs and reading several books, I came to believe the astral body was not solid. As a result, I started having experiences like the following:

02/23/80—OBE #9

. . . Another strange thing about this morning's projection was: I folded my arms around my chest to rest them, but they went right through my chest! They rested on the bed.

This example shows the malleability of the astral body: I folded my arms through my chest instead of on top of it.

Some people can travel just by thinking of a person or place. But it's not always that simple. It's not just the thought that makes us travel but our beliefs too. In *Journeys Out of the Body*, Robert Monroe wasn't always able to travel to a desired person or place. When trying to contact a friend, he often found himself in unexpected, unfamiliar surroundings.

I've also run into these problems, which I think stemmed mainly from my beliefs. I couldn't rationalize how people could move from place to place during OBEs, and my doubts and skepticism got in my way. I harbored a belief that it takes more than thoughts to travel. Limiting beliefs such as these can cause us a great deal of trouble. Here is an example:

12/22/85 Sun—OBE #120

. . . Annoyed, I closed my eyes again, sat up again, turned, and stood up again. This time I walked blindly through the door into the living room. I walked across the living room, almost to the door of the apartment. I thought, "I'm far enough away from my body now; it should be safe to open my eyes." I opened my eyes, and again I was transported back to the same position just above the body.

I figured this was happening because of some belief I harbored, so I decided to combat the belief. As I lay there, I thought strongly, "I am the master of my reality, and I control what happens here." With that thought, I felt a strong sensation like a vibration sweeping into me, giving me a sense of power.

I thought, "Good. Now, I will raise myself up with the power of my thoughts." I used my mind to pull up, and I started forcefully rising up one-half foot . . . one foot . . . one and one-half feet. Then I questioned whether it ought to work, since I hadn't had much luck in the past with this method. That doubt caused me to stop rising, and I started gently bobbing up and down, as if my conflicting beliefs were fighting each other, one pulling me up, the other pushing me down. Then I blacked out.

The following experience illustrates further how we can use one set of beliefs to combat another:

04/13/86 Sun—OBE #125

This morning I was trying to sleep but kept thinking about trying to leave my body. As I was heading toward sleep, I found myself in a very good condition for OBEs. I was lying on my left side. Very easily I started swaying back and forth in my body as described before. I swayed back and forth and slipped outside my body. I thought, "Well, that was easy enough." I slipped a little bit backward and found myself stuck to the body. I tried to pry myself away but was unsuccessful. I closed my eyes and said aloud, "I am in complete control of this reality while I am out of my body. If I am stuck, it's because I believe I am stuck. And I no longer want to be stuck." I opened my eyes again and tried once more to pry myself away, also without success.

I decided to try something different. My body was near the edge of the bed. I reasoned that if I was close to the edge of the bed and pushed myself off, I would fall off the bed, thus freeing myself from the body. I was using my own beliefs to free myself: I knew I had a belief that I would fall off the bed. This belief was stronger than my belief that I was stuck to my body. I rolled a little bit until I was lying on my back (my body was still on its left side). I wanted to fall gently, so I gently fell to the ground and I felt a sharp—but not painful—jab in my back caused by hitting something on the floor next to my bed.

The point is, if you are planning to attempt OBEs, it's very helpful, before you set out on your adventure, to examine your desires, beliefs, fears, and expectations about the experience.

EXERCISE 22
Buzzing

This exercise is similar to the musical imagination exercise. Relax completely, then try to get to that passive, quiescent frame of mind.

As vividly as you can, imagine there is a coarse buzzing sound in your head. Pretend the buzzing is just a little bit too quiet to hear, but getting louder. Simultaneously listen intently for the buzzing to become loud enough to hear.

As the buzzing becomes louder, imagine the sound is causing your soul to vibrate. Increase the imaginary sound until you feel as if your soul is being rattled and shaken to the core. Hold the imaginary buzzing and vibrating for several minutes.

Repeat the procedure several times if necessary.

23

Environmental Factors

For a long time I tried to find out if out-of-body experiences are influenced by environmental factors, such as weather, moon cycles, biorhythms, etc. I usually kept good records of my OBEs so that I could study these variables. Here is what I found.

Weather

Weather doesn't seem to influence my ability to have OBEs. I've lived in Arizona as well as Minnesota, and I've induced OBEs when outside temperatures were near -30°F and also when outside temperatures were near +115°F. However, if my body is too hot or cold, it's hard for me to achieve the focus needed to induce an OBE. It doesn't seem to matter if it's raining, snowing, or sunny.

Moon Cycles

Some people believe that the moon can affect our ability to induce OBEs, but I think that's a myth. I studied the moon cycles a long time and found no influence. I've had OBEs under full moons, new moons, and everything between. For one period of study that spanned more than a year and a half, I averaged a 58 percent full moon.

Biorhythms

For a long time I kept track of my biorhythms, in the hopes that I would find a correlation between OBEs and biorhythms. Biorhythms didn't seem to make a difference. I've had OBEs on physical, emotional, and intellectual "critical" days. I've also had OBEs when these influences were farthest from their "critical" period.

Months of the Year

I've had OBEs in all months of the year. Strangely, I usually have fewer OBEs in July. I suspect that's because July is when I have the least amount of time to practice.

Days of the Week

I've had OBEs on every day of the week, but I've had many more OBEs on Saturdays and Sundays. That is because I have the time to practice then. On the weekend, I can stay in bed late and induce OBEs once my body is fully rested and relaxed. During the week, I don't normally have the time required to induce OBEs.

Special Days

Halloween is traditionally considered a special day, the day that spirits can influence and communicate with the physical world. Other days such as Christmas, Easter, and Thanksgiving have special meanings for various groups of people. These special days can evoke feelings in believers; fear on Halloween, peace on Christmas, worship on Easter. Do the collective feelings of these people affect our ability to leave the body? As far as I can tell, no. What about the emotions we have on these days? To some degree, I believe our emotions do have an effect. Once, I was uncomfortable about leaving my body on Halloween because I thought it would be a perfect opportunity for spirits to possess my body. But I did it anyway, and there were no complications.

Prior Amount of Sleep

I've had OBEs with various amounts of sleep. I recommend getting lots of sleep before you try to have OBEs. One of the biggest problems is trying to induce OBEs when the body is too tired.

Prior Music Listening Habits

Music relaxes my consciousness too quickly to induce an OBE. During practice, I like to hold on to the edge of consciousness as long as I can. If I listen to music, I get distracted by it and drop off quickly to sleep. Therefore, I recommend silence.

Food

As far as I can tell, food has absolutely no influence on my ability to have OBEs. However, people have reported that fasting can increase the ability to have OBEs. I've never tried fasting. Some people believe that vegetarianism is better for OBEs. I've tried a vegetarian diet (except for eating dairy products), and it didn't seem to make a difference.

Liquids

I haven't found any correlation between my intake of liquids and my ability to have OBEs. I do recommend avoiding alcoholic beverages before trying to induce OBEs. Alcohol unfocuses your mind. Believe me, you need as much focus as possible. Sylvan Muldoon recommended jarring your subconscious into taking you out of body by making yourself as thirsty as possible. Muldoon claimed that if you go to bed very thirsty, your subconscious will sometimes "sleepwalk" astrally toward a source of water. In other words, your subconscious detects the thirst, and tries to satisfy it subconsciously because you refuse to do it consciously. I've never tried this method.

Reading

Reading OBE books does influence my ability to have OBEs. When I read a book about OBEs, I focus my full attention on the topic while I'm reading, and that sends a message to my subconscious, saying "let me out!" And it does.

Direction

In *Journeys Out of the Body*, Robert Monroe recommended pointing your body north when trying to induce OBEs, I've tried to have OBEs facing all directions, and I've been successful in all directions. Strangely enough, I have my best luck when my body is pointing west. I have my worst luck when my body is pointing north. When I induced the vibrations the first time, my body was pointing west. Perhaps it's more effective to point the direction you did during your first successful experience.

Practice

By far, the biggest influence on my ability to have OBEs has been the amount of time I spend practicing it.

EXERCISE 23
A High-Pitched Whining

During your OBE practice sessions, you may have noticed a high-pitched whining noise in your head. If you listen closely, you will notice the noise I'm referring to. We all hear this high-pitched sound constantly, but normally the sound is drowned out by constant distractions and sounds all around us. Most people don't notice it, but some people have a disorder called tinnitus, which causes this sound to be unusually loud and distracting. You can use this sound to induce OBEs.

For this exercise, relax and focus your mind as before. Then start listening for this whining sound in your head. Once you find it, use your imagination to try to increase the pitch and volume. Increase the pitch until the sound is almost out of the range of your hearing. This can cause the vibrations to sweep in and free you from your body.

Personally, I think the sound has nothing to do with the vibrations. This exercise is effective only because it can teach you how to properly focus your mind.

24

How to Have an OBE

Many people try to induce OBEs without success because they don't know what to do. Unfortunately, most books on the subject don't contain instructions. The few books that contain instructions are typically vague and incomplete. In the exercises given with each chapter, I have already suggested many things to try. In this chapter, I want to fill in some of the gaps and also provide a detailed description of my most successful method. Of course, I can't guarantee positive results. Your success depends on the quality and quantity of the effort you put forth.

Conditioning

Most OBE authors agree that your subconscious takes you out of your body every night. With practice you can use this to your advantage: you can train your subconscious to "wake you up" after it has left the body. I have used many methods for impressing this idea on my subconscious: affirmations, reading books, listening to subliminal OBE suggestion tapes, playful visualizations, and listening to music that has OBE-suggestive words.

The first method, affirmations or self-suggestion, is to tell yourself, "Tonight I will have an out-of-body experience," or similar suggestions. The best times to do this are right before you fall asleep and especially right after you wake up in the morning. At these times you are in close contact with your subconscious. I wake up very slowly. For about a half hour I'm in contact with my subconscious mind. When I give myself suggestions then, they are very effective. Make these affirmations several times a day.

The second method is to read OBE books. I usually have more OBEs when I've recently been reading a book on astral projection. Reading about OBEs and thinking about them as you read makes an impression on your subconscious mind that can often be more effective than self-suggestion.

The third method is to use suggestion tapes. The Monroe Institute now has sets of "Gateway" tapes to aid the would-be astral traveler. Valley of the Sun Publishing has a set called "Astral Projection" which contains one hypnosis tape and one subliminal suggestion tape. Other tapes are also available.

The fourth method is to use playful imagination. Affirmations that use visualization are even better than verbal affirmations. Visualize yourself separating from the body. As you do, think to yourself, "Yes, I can do that." Imagine elaborate scenes where you are either flying through valleys like a glider or shooting away from your body into outer space. Again, this should be done frequently throughout the day, and especially right after you wake up in the morning.

The fifth method is to listen to music with words that suggest OBEs. I made a tape for myself, full of such songs by various artists. The songs might not be about

OBEs, but they still remind me of them enough to make an impression on my subconscious mind. Some examples are: "Kashmir" by Led Zeppelin, "Astral Traveler" by Yes, "The Wall" by Kansas, "Lights" by Styx, "Fly By Night" by Rush, and "Backwards Traveler" by Paul McCartney.

Physical Preparation

The best time to attempt an OBE is in the morning, after you have awakened naturally (i.e., not from an alarm clock). Since most of us work during the week, it's easier to try on the weekends. Give your body plenty of rest. Each person needs a different amount of sleep. The trick is to make your body tired enough to stay in a relaxed state, but not too tired. If I don't sleep enough, I'm too tired and fall back into a deep sleep while practicing. If I oversleep and then practice, I am too wide awake and can't focus well. The body should be well rested but relaxed, and the mind must be alert.

When the time comes to practice, try to detect how tired you are. If you're too tired, stretch a little in bed or shake the sleep off. You may want to get up first and have a cup of coffee. This will usually keep you from falling back to sleep during practice. It is better to wake yourself up completely before starting.

Music is wonderful for relaxation and calming the mind. It's okay to listen to relaxing music during your OBE practice, but this can also work against you: listening to external sounds can distract you from focusing inward. Also, if you listen to music before bedtime, you may be too relaxed and sleepy to practice the next morning.

When you practice, make sure you have good circulation. Get into a position where your limbs won't "fall asleep" because of poor circulation.

Make sure you won't be distracted during practice. Keep your windows closed to keep noises out, unplug the telephone, turn off all televisions, radios, and other noisy things. Don't set any time limits on your practice. It is counter-productive to check the time and wonder if your time limit is up. Also, make sure your bladder is empty before practice; the need to go to the bathroom can ruin a good practice.

Step I. Relaxation

The next important condition for OBE induction is a completely relaxed physical body. Relaxation is important because if you aren't relaxed, you'll have too much consciousness focused in your body. Laboratory tests on astral travelers have shown (with the help of BSR and GSR skin resistance monitors) that the physical body is more relaxed during an OBE than during sleep. Ideally, your physical body should be completely relaxed in every respect during practice. I recommend practicing relaxation every day until you can completely relax your physical body in a few minutes.

Relax your body from limb to limb, working from your feet up to your head, until even your face is completely relaxed. Use any technique you are comfortable with to relax completely. If you don't know any relaxation techniques, do this: Systematically tighten each muscle and make it tense until there is a slight fatigue, then let go and feel the muscle relax. After you've relaxed every muscle, start over and check every muscle again.

You may notice that the more relaxed your body is, the less you can actually "feel" it. Encourage this feeling: while you're relaxing, pretend as vividly as you can that you do not have your left arm; as if it's been cut off and you can't feel it. When the sensation of having no arm becomes quite real to you, that arm is very relaxed. Next, pretend that your other arm does not exist. Next, your legs. Have some playful fun by pretending that your arms are in different positions, and see how vividly you can imagine these things. If you are able to lose all feeling in your arms and legs, or imagine that they are in different positions, your body is very relaxed.

Next, relax your face completely. Here's one way to relax your face: with your eyes closed, stare deeper and deeper into the blackness, while *very slowly* tightening your eyebrows and rolling your eyes up slightly until your eyebrow muscles become tired. Then completely relax your facial muscles for about 15 seconds. Repeat the process again until your eyebrow muscles are tired again, then relax again for another 15 seconds. Repeat this process about six or seven times. Completely relax your whole body again, and then try to make your mind blank and relaxed too. The vibrations may even come at this point, making the rest of the process unnecessary! After you're completely relaxed, pay no more attention to your body.

Step 2. Quiesce and Focus Your Mind

This is *the single most important step*. There are five key points to focusing your mind for OBE induction. They are: state of mind, realism, motion, receptivity, and passivity.

When you are trying to leave your body, the most important thing is your state of mind. When I've been in an "ideal" state of mind, leaving my body seems like child's play, as easy and natural as breathing. But when I'm not in that state of mind, it seems very difficult. I can't "teach" this state of mind, but I can describe what it's like. Once you've experienced astral projection, you'll know what state of mind to aim for. The best state of mind is one in which you are a quiet, completely passive, single-minded observer. In this passive state, your mind does not wander. You are not emotional. You are not analytical either. You are merely an observer. Visualization is important in many OBE techniques, and this passive state of mind makes it easier to visualize images a long time without your mind wandering.

The second point, realism, has to do with the degree of focus. This world seems real to us because we are so focused here. You should learn to focus outside your body to such a degree that it all becomes real. Focus your mind into that single thread of consciousness.

The third point, motion, concerns the swaying motion you feel within your body. I start an inner "swaying" sensation in my imagination that later becomes quite real. Then I use the momentum of the swaying to propel myself out of my body. Pretend that your body is gently swaying back and forth, or left to right in a regular motion. Try to make this swaying feeling as vivid as possible.

The fourth point is receptivity. This receptive state of mind is important in calling or inducing the vibrations. You should learn to make yourself receptive to whatever comes during practice.

The fifth point, passivity, is also very important. The more passive you are, the easier it is to enter the OBE state. As long as you have a conscious "controlling interest" in your experience, you are too focused in this reality. Develop the attitude of doing the exercises, not because you are *interested* in watching them, but just for passive reasons: just to see what happens next, or just for the sake

Out of Body Experiences

of doing it. While practicing, you should be concerned only with the current moment in time. Be accepting of what comes. Try to assume an attitude where you really don't care what will happen. Be completely in the present moment, with no thoughts of what will happen next. *The American Heritage Dictionary* defines "passive" as

> 1. Receiving or subjected to an action without responding or initiating an action in return. 2. Accepting without objection or resistance; compliant. 3. Not participating, acting, or operating; inert . . .

By this definition, you should be in a state where you can be subjected to weird feelings without responding, physically or mentally. No matter what hits you, you should be in such a passive state that, when something hits you, you think, "Oh. That's nice," and just continue to lie there and visualize.

In this passive state, you can initiate actions (like the visualizations) without responding to them. You fall asleep by becoming interested in, and responding to, your own thoughts and visualizations. If you can initiate that state and keep your consciousness out of that dream-trap, you can retain your consciousness after it leaves your body. You just want to become a passive observer.

I've talked before about needing to suspend a certain portion of your consciousness to leave your body. Suspend the portion that has a vested interest in what's happening.

Slow your thoughts and bring yourself into that passive and receptive state of mind. Clear your mind of all thoughts: there are many techniques for doing this. If you don't have a method, try the following: With your eyes closed, pretend that you're looking for something that might appear directly in front of you. Just quietly watch your mental viewing screen. Stare into the blackness.

Step 3. Wander on the Edge of Consciousness

The next step is to "wander on the edge of consciousness," exploring the border between waking and sleeping. Allow yourself to start falling asleep, but then "catch" yourself, rouse yourself again, and make sure you're fully conscious. Let yourself start to fall asleep again, this time allowing yourself to get a little closer toward sleep, then rouse yourself again. Do this several times until your body is very relaxed and your mind is in that "passive" framework that I discussed.

Step 4. Visualize an Object

At this point, you will probably notice occasional hypnogogic images, but be sure to maintain a level of conscious awareness.

Next, visualize any small object, such as a small cube, about six feet directly in front of your face. It is even better to wait for a hypnogogic image of an object, then use visualization to take control of it. Visualize it as clearly as you can. Don't continue until you can see this object clearly in your mind's eye.

Step 5. Sway the Object a Small Amount

Then begin to move the object up and down so that it appears to come a little bit closer to you and then moves back to where it began. At first, visualize only a tiny amount of movement, as if the object is merely slowly swaying toward you and away from you.

Keep the object swaying constantly. Don't let it stop moving. Keeping the object in motion will help to stabilize the image in your mind and give it more realism.

Step 6. Increase the Amount of Swaying

Slowly increase the distance the object sways. Keep swinging the image back and forth toward you, each time bringing it a bit closer to you. As you do this, the image may seem to become more real. Make sure your visualization has a sense of perspective and depth. Each time the object comes closer, it should look bigger. Each time the object pulls away, it should look smaller.

Remember, you must also keep that passive, quiescent state of mind during the entire exercise.

Step 7. Sway Opposite to the Object

Try to feel as if you are swaying in the opposite direction of the object. Imagine that the object has a strong gravity that affects your swaying. As the object swings closer to you, you are pulled toward it. As it swings away from you, you sway back to your original position within your body.

As the object gets closer and closer with each swing, feel its gravity pull you more and more in its direction.

Step 8. Grab the Object and Let It Pull You Out

After the image becomes very vivid, when it swings close to you, "grab" onto the image with your mind. As the image swings away, your consciousness will follow it and be pulled away from your body.

At this point you will be out of your body. Then you can "let go" of that quiesced state of mind, expand your consciousness, and you will be very wide awake and very alert. You are then free to explore the nonphysical world!

It is important to examine your consciousness during the experience to make sure that you are not dreaming. During the experience, ask yourself, "Is this really happening, or is it a dream?" After you return to your body, recall how conscious you were during the experience.

Learning to leave your body is something that takes a lot of time, practice, and patience. Don't expect results overnight. This chapter has a lot of information to absorb at once. You may spend several attempts just trying to remember all the subtleties involved. Some people don't have any OBEs until they have spent years trying. And some people don't get results because they try too hard; learn to let go. The good news is, the first OBE is the hardest. Once you've had an OBE, it's easier to induce more.

Also, don't be afraid to experiment and try new things. Develop your own techniques. Use whatever works best for you.

25

Psychic Experiences

As I continued to practice out-of-body experiences, I had more and more psychic experiences. And I was trying to deny it all. I didn't consider myself psychic, but psychic experiences kept piling up, one upon another, forcing me to admit that I had psychic abilities. What's more, psychic things happened so often that I couldn't write them off as coincidence. I felt as if my higher self was combating my skepticism by throwing undeniable, unbelievable things in my face.

I had many different types of psychic experiences. Remarkably, they all seemed to happen overnight. As crazy as it sounds, wishes started coming true. Suddenly the world was magical.

Telepathy

Suddenly I was "taking the words out of people's mouths," not weekly or daily, but hourly! I wrote down some of these experiences in my journals. Here are some examples:

05/12/80 Mon

. . . I asked my mom what we were having for lunch. The word "tuna fish" came to me. A while later she said, "There might be some tuna fish around."

05/20/80

Today JF and I were talking about how neat it would be if BS (our English teacher) were also our computer-science teacher. I *thought*, "What was BS's major in college?" JF suddenly *said*, "He was a physics major."

10/14/83 Fri

. . . For one of my classes this quarter, I am on a team of five people working on a computer project. Today we had to think of a name for our team. I suggested the name "Magnum Opus," and right away one of my teammates said he had just been thinking that and was about to suggest it himself!

10/04/85 Fri

. . . I was programming busily, when I thought I heard JP ask about my computer program (whether I fixed my ENDIF statements in a particular section of code). I started explaining to him that I did, and what else I had done, when he told me that he never asked the question! He only *thought* about asking me! And yet I answered him as if he had asked the question he had in his mind.

Telepathic Sending

This is similar to telepathy, except you are deliberately trying to send a message to another person. Another term might be "remote suggestion." This is the ability to put thoughts or suggestions into the minds of others. A good example was the incident in which I suggested that my bus driver speed up. Here are more examples:

08/20/80 Wed

I went to Burger King for lunch. With my lunch I ordered some french fries. When the server went to get my fries, I telepathed, "Give me a few more." Right before my eyes, she turned around, reached in the bin and added more fries to my order! The french fries were already measured into bags. But she grabbed a bag and then she added some to my bag of fries! I said aloud, "I don't believe it!"

03/19/81 Thu

. . . I was eating supper with my Dad and I wanted a napkin. I decided to do a psychic experiment. I tried to put the word "napkin" into my Dad's mind. A little while later, he reached up and grabbed a napkin for me. That's not too strange. But then he asked, "Were you just thinking 'napkin'?" Then I told him about my experiment.

10/21/85 Mon

. . . PF is a local computer dealer. During the previous week, he had ordered some computers from our company. He never went through with his order, and all of us wanted DB to call PF and ask him about his order. DB didn't want to call PF back. At a particular time in the day, I said to everyone, "Since DB doesn't want to call PF, we'll have to get PF to call us!" JS asked, "How are we going to do that?" I replied, "Well, we'll think about him really hard, and then he'll pick up on it and call us." Amused, JS said, "Okay." A few minutes later, PF called, after about a week of not hearing from him. JS said, "It worked!"

Clairvoyance

Clairvoyance is the power to perceive something out of the range of our senses. For instance, it was common for me to "know" what song was playing on the radio before I turned it on, or to "hear" the next song to be played, before the current song was over. It was common for me to brush these experiences off as "coincidence" to a certain point, but when these coincidences started stacking up, I started writing them down in my journals. I couldn't ignore them any longer.

This ability was very helpful. Often I knew when the telephone would ring. Sometimes I would also know who was calling, which helped me avoid people I didn't want to talk to. In playing cards, I would "know" which card was best for me to play, without knowing or needing to know what the other players had. Sometimes I had fun with this ability. Here is an example:

05/31/84 Thu

. . . I was talking with my friend and fellow programmer, WB, about names. He said, "I bet you could never guess my middle name—it's so strange." I calmly said, "Otto," and he said "Wow! How did you know? I never told that to anyone, and it isn't on my job application or W-4 forms either!" Then he said, "But I got another middle name, but you'd never guess this other one in a million years." I calmly said, "Gerhard?" to which he replied, "How did you know that? That's not a common name!" I just said, "Just a guess," to which he replied, "I don't believe it!"

Visions

Although visions are similar to clairvoyance, I list them separately because there is a difference. With clairvoyance, I just seemed to "know" things out of the reach of my senses, but with visions, I saw clear-as-day pictures in front of me. I had to draw my own conclusions from those visions. Here's an example:

05/06/80 *Tue*

A couple of weeks ago, I was going to sleep one night and . . . suddenly I saw a vision. In the vision I saw a very clear picture of my Aunt K. lying down with her eyes closed. I knew she wasn't dead, but asleep or passed out in the vision. When it was over, I got out of bed and walked to the living room where my mom was reading. I asked her, "How is Aunt K.?" She said, "Why?" I told her of my vision, and she said that she hadn't talked to Aunt K. for a long time.

Last Friday I heard the story. Aunt K. fell out of bed one night. When she fell, she hit her head, and for a while she was blinded. Now she is out of the hospital after several days and is recovering her sight.

As close as I can tell, the vision took place on or near the day of her accident.

Psychic Dreams

I discovered that dreams can be a source of psychic information. On 08/02/81, I had a dream that started normally: I was at the university bookstore. Then the dream took on a strange quality, and I was paged to come to the information desk. At the information desk, a lady handed me a telephone. A woman's voice told me I should come home because there had been a death in my family. I asked the woman who had died, but she said she couldn't tell me; all she could tell me was the person's social security number over the phone. When she told me the Social Security number, I "knew" it was my father who had "died" in my dream. I was shocked and sad, so I consciously decided to end the dream (which led me to an OBE). My father was in perfect health, but not for long. This was the first "warning" I was given about my father's death.

Precognition

Precognition could also be classified as clairvoyance, but instead of the ability to "know" the present, this is the ability to "know" the future. On November 2, 1981, I had a certain "feeling" or "knowing" that my father was soon to die. I wrote it down, but I didn't tell anyone my feeling. My father was still in good health. Soon after that, my dad became ill and died on January 13, 1982. A better example of precognition is the following:

11/26/80 Wed

I took a 94B bus home from work today. On the bus ride to downtown Minneapolis, I thought about many things, but the main thought that kept nagging me the whole way home was: "I'd better relax more, in case we get in an accident." I would feel the need for relaxation, then I would realize I was tense, then I would relax again. When I'd tense up again, I'd tell myself to relax again, and so on. The thoughts kept nagging me until I decided to pursue them. I thought about the prospect of my bus being in an accident. I kept reassuring myself, "No way could it happen." But the thought nagged. I looked around me to see how cushioned I'd be if I were to get in an accident. I was sitting sideways, next to another man who would cushion me in an accident. I looked to see how everyone else was cushioned. There was only one person better cushioned than I. I thought about having an accident for about five to ten minutes. Then I relaxed a final time, and I stayed relaxed for the rest of the bus ride. Sure enough, my bus then hit a van from behind.

Déjà Vu

Déjà vu is similar to precognition; you have a certain sense of knowing what the future will be, but there is also an overwhelming sense of having done it all before. It is as if the whole scene was rehearsed countless times in the past. It is typical to ask yourself, "Haven't I done this before?" These experiences tie into psychic dreams. Here is an example from my journals.

07/05/84 Thu

I've had two déjà vu experiences recently. The first I'll mention was today. I was at work, at CC's terminal. CC was on the phone, and I knew every word she was going to say before she said it. I broke out laughing, but she didn't understand why I was laughing.

The other experience was last Tuesday. Again I was at work talking to SB about the BASIC computer language when I remembered I had done this once before in a dream, and I knew everything SB was going to say. In the dream, my boss DJ walked in and saw me talking with SB about BASIC. I was embarrassed because I don't normally use BASIC in my work. I thought, "Oh, no! DJ will be coming in here any instant, and I'll have to explain myself. I've got to get out of here fast!" So I tried to excuse myself and leave. But when I tried to leave, SB asked me some question, which delayed me further. I answered and tried to leave again. He stopped me again saying, "Hang on, let me show you something." I tried to escape a third time and fourth time, but each time SB came up with a reason to keep me there. Then DJ came in the room and said the same thing he said in my dream. I was indeed embarrassed, and I had to explain my interest in BASIC and how it pertains to my current work.

The example mentioned above lasted a long time—about twenty minutes. Both experiences were "remembered" from a dream. At times I would dream the future quite often, and the dreams would give me a déjà vu experience later. My personal belief is that we use our dreams sometimes to *plan* the future. The dreams were the plans, and the plans were carried out perfectly. In these cases, my efforts to change the planned events were continually thwarted.

Apparitions

The main problem I had with most of my psychic experiences is that they were not very concrete. Often they were just "feelings" I had about situations, or "stray" thoughts in my mind. I had a hard time believing in these phenomena. I found out there were other, more concrete types of psychic phenomena, such as apparitions. An apparition is the physical appearance of a nonphysical entity or object. The following is an example.

Out of Body Experiences

08/19/83 Fri

Wednesday I had read an article in *The Encyclopedia of Occultism and Parapsychology* on the subject of medium-ship. The article talked about physical manifestations of all sorts, and I was interested in it. I wished right then that some spirits would do a physical manifestation, to prove their existence to me.

Later that night I woke up startled, with a sense of danger. I opened my eyes, and much to my shock, I saw a hand materialized in midair near my head, and the hand held something. I was so shocked and frightened that I jumped and shook the bed violently. Whatever was in the hand went flying, and the hand withdrew from me and went up and disintegrated. I fainted, and my consciousness gradually fell into nothingness, although there was a slight delay.

Psychokinesis (PK) or Telekinesis (TK)

Psychokinesis is the physical movement or alteration of an object by psychic means. One day I had just left my place of work at about 8:00 P.M. I was very excited about many things. The book I was reading was exciting, I recently had had an exciting OBE, and other exciting things were happening. For some reason, as I waited to catch my bus, I felt very psychically strong. I felt as if I could do anything. I'm never idle with such feelings; I had to find some way to test out this feeling of power. I looked around for nearby objects. "If I really have this power," I reasoned to myself, "I can probably walk over to any parking meter and open it up with my mind." I walked over to a random parking meter, slipped my hands gently around it, and it opened effortlessly! Shiny coins spilled all over the ground. For a second or two I stood there in shock. What if someone saw me? What should I do? I am a very honest person. I tried to close the meter, but spilled coins were preventing the door from closing. I quickly cleared it out, closed the door, and started frantically plugging coins into the meter. Occasional drivers must have thought I was crazy, plugging handfuls of coins into a parking meter, long after parking hours—especially since there wasn't a car in that spot! I picked up all the coins from the ground and plugged them one by one into the meter. My heart was still pounding as I got on the bus, and a long time after that.

Here is another example from my journal:

09/24/84 Mon

Weird things are starting to happen again. After work I wanted to do some drawing, but I haven't seen my drawing pencil since our trip. I tried unsuccessfully to find the pencil many times since. The last time I looked was Saturday when I searched the house and JP's apartment.

Today I searched again for it, but without success, and while I was searching, my inner voice said, "try using your psi to find it." I didn't find it, so JP and I decided to go shopping for one. Before we left, I sat in the middle of his living room next to the biggest chair, waiting for him to get ready.

We went shopping, but I didn't buy a new pencil since JP offered to lend me one. When we got home, I went up to JP's apartment. While he got on the phone, I wandered into the middle of his living room. There, in the middle of JP's biggest chair was my drawing pencil! I asked JP about it, but he said it was impossible because he had been sitting on that chair just before we left! Therefore, before we left the pencil had not been on the chair, or in fact, anywhere to be found. But when we returned, the pencil was lying on the chair. There is absolutely no possible explanation of how that pencil appeared there or where it came from. It *had* to have been teleported there because JP was never out of my sight from the time we left until the time we returned. That chair was empty when we left.

Clairaudience

Clairaudience is the ability to hear voices of people who are not physically present. Experience would suggest this can happen between two living persons as well as the traditional "spirit voices." This is different from telepathy. In telepathy you "pick up" the thoughts of others. In clairaudience, you hear a voice as plain as day. When it has happened to me, it's been so loud and clear that I've looked around to see who was speaking, but no one was in sight. Here are two good examples:

10/14/83 Fri

One other remarkable thing happened a couple of weeks ago. I was at the university campus, walking to one of my classes, and I was thinking about an article in *The Encyclopedia of Occultism and Parapsychology* that said the term "inner voice" refers to clairaudience. Suddenly I spiritually heard a female voice. The voice said, "My name is Julia, and I say it's not important where the wisdom comes from, but rather, it's the wisdom itself that counts!" That was the first time I ever heard a voice that claimed to have a name! Also, that voice didn't need translation like my inner voice does. Instead, the words came through directly. Naturally, it shocked me quite a lot.

07/05/84 *Thu*

Today I was working at one of my employer's customer sites. I had arranged for SO to meet me at P Company at 6:00 P.M. At 5:40 P.M. I looked at my watch and thought, "I have plenty of time; SO won't be here for twenty minutes." So I started entering data into their computer. At 5:45 P.M. I heard SO's voice—loud and clear—yelling something like, "Hello? Anyone there?" I couldn't believe SO would be there so early, yet I heard his voice. It sounded as if he were yelling from outside, yet I was sitting in the Parts Room in the middle of a big building. All the windows were closed and locked about a hundred feet away.

I ran to the big doors, opened them, and ran outside, only to find SO just getting off his motorcycle, taking off his (full) helmet. I asked him if he had yelled anything and he said he hadn't; he had just now arrived. He said he tried to mentally send the message to me! I checked; there was no way he could have yelled loud enough for me to hear him in the Parts Room (especially with his motorcycle helmet on!). The alarming thing about this was the clarity of his "voice." It sounded as plain as day. I should also mention that I had a radio playing at the time, and I "heard" his voice over the sound of the radio. It was that clear. SO remarked, "Either you're very sensitive, or I'm a very strong transmitter."

Other Experiences

Some experiences just don't quite fit into any categories. Here are a few examples:

09/27/80 *Sat*

A large moth came into my bedroom. I mentally commanded it to enter my cupped hands. It immediately fluttered directly into my hands, and I cupped my hands around it. Then I promptly ushered it out of the house without harming it.

04/17/81 *Fri*

For some reason or another, I was trying to think of the German word for "tired." I wracked my brain. I was still trying to remember it when I heard myself physically say "müde!" Then I thought, "Yeah, that's it." Then I realized what had happened. I remembered the word only because my body had just said it. I had no intention of saying anything, nor did I remember the word until *after* I said it. Weird!

Conclusions

Of course, there are also many psychic things I haven't experienced. I've never experienced mediumship, automatic writing, or anything like that.

When most of these experiences were happening to me, I wasn't really expecting them or even wanting them. I wanted OBEs because they were concrete and indisputable in my own mind. They couldn't be brushed off as coincidences or delusions of grandeur. They were undeniably real to me as a participant. Still, when I practiced my OBE techniques, I was exploring altered states of consciousness and meditation. And that was enough to unlock all these other "psychic" experiences, and more.

Therefore, I warn you: if you do plan to try out-of-body experiences for yourself, be prepared for a possible barrage of other psychic experiences. On the other hand, if your aim is to develop psychic abilities, practicing OBE techniques may work well. You may get a few OBEs out of the deal too!

The possibilities of psychic experience are as wide and varied as normal experience. But a person's psychic abilities don't make him or her more spiritual or better than anyone else. Rather than aiming to induce out-of-body experiences or psychic experiences, I would prefer that you strive for spiritual growth (whatever that means to you). I believe that working on your own spiritual growth will naturally make you more psychic as you progress.

EXERCISE 25
Developing Psychic Skills

As I learned more about psychic experiences, I discovered that my psychic abilities fade in and out in cycles. At times they are strong, and at other times they seemed to fade out completely. I also learned that it's possible to increase psychic abilities. Here are some exercises that may increase your psychic abilities.

- Practice meditation and OBEs.

- Give yourself suggestions just before sleep and when you first wake up. For example: "I am psychic."

- Visualize yourself pouring love out in all directions.

- Imagine extending your awareness until you're trying to feel the emotions of your whole neighborhood.

- Try musical meditation and listening to hypnotic songs.

- Give yourself reminders ("post-it" notes or whatever) with messages like, "I am psychic" or, "I can leave my body."

- Make pacts with your higher self. Here is an example.

  I am psychic. I know that the universe responds to my needs and desires quickly and completely. In return, I promise to cooperate with my oversoul, follow impulses, act on intuitions, share knowledge, spread love, and cooperate with my higher self.

26

Questions and Answers

Certain questions are frequently asked about the out-of-body experience. Here is how I would answer them, in no particular order:

What do you do during an OBE?
Mostly, I explore. I experiment. I have an insatiable curiosity, so I just go out and try things. I also love to fly.

Can you lose your body?
If anyone has lost his or her body, they obviously haven't lived to tell about it. But all indications are that you can't lose your body for good. I believe that your oversoul has invested a great deal of time and energy in creating and maintaining a physical body for a purpose. Your oversoul is not going to give up your body until your purpose has been fulfilled. Thousands of people have experienced OBEs and wandered thousands of miles away from their body. After a certain period, they usually just lose consciousness and find themselves back in their body again.

What about possession?

Perhaps if you have mediumistic tendencies, spirits can temporarily inhabit your body while you are out. However, spirits cannot possess your body long term unless you give them permission to do so. My clairvoyant friend, LD, told me of an OBE during which the spirit of a woman entered her body without permission. The woman was trying to animate LD's body but couldn't. LD returned to her body to find it occupied. She was so angry that she yelled at the spirit to get out "or else." The spirit said no, but LD got furious and yelled "Now!" The unhappy spirit quickly left the body, and LD entered it again. The point is, even when you are out of your body, your oversoul has a "claim" on that body. Other spirits do not have the power to animate your body.

Can you encounter something evil like a demon?

I don't believe in evil. There are only two kinds of demons. The first is the demon we create from our own fears. If you don't believe in evil, you cannot encounter these demons. If you understand and face your fears, you can face these demons and destroy them with an act of will. The only thing you have to fear is fear itself.

The second kind is the spirit of a dead person who is playing the role of a demon to make him/herself appear more intimidating. But that's different from evil. Remember this: they are just spirits like you and I. They have no more power than you do, despite how they look or act. If you are a gentle soul, just visualize a white light around the spirit and send feelings of love to the poor misguided spirit. If you're ornery, tell them to stick it where the sun doesn't shine, and walk away. If you're playful, make yourself into a big demon and give them their own treatment.

They can't harm you, and they can't possess your body unless you give them power over you by being afraid.

What are the psychological effects? Can you go insane?
Again, I can speak only from personal experience. One common definition of "sane" is a person who is integrated and functioning normally in society. I can say this much: I haven't had any problems holding a job. As a computer programmer and analyst, stress levels are high and my brain functions are constantly being taxed. My OBEs haven't done any noticeable harm.

There is an excellent book called *With the Eyes of the Mind* by Gabbard and Twemlow that contains an in-depth study of the psychology of OBEs. It compares the OBE to other psychological phenomena. In short, they found that the OBE shouldn't be grouped with psychological disorders such as dissociation, schizophrenia, autoscopy, and other body boundary disturbances. OBE falls into a category of its own.

When is the best time to practice?
The best time to practice is in the morning, when you are awake, refreshed, and not likely to fall asleep. I mostly practice Saturday and Sunday mornings because I can sleep in late, wake up refreshed and then have plenty of time to practice. I also recommend you take a nap some-time during the day, and use that time to attempt to leave your body. Naps are better than bedtime because you're usually not as tired. You can relax and really get into it, without being so tired that you just fall asleep right away. If you only practice before bedtime, make sure to go to bed early so you won't fall asleep immediately.

What's the difference between an OBE and a lucid dream?

Some people believe that OBEs are the same thing as lucid dreams. It's easy to confuse the two. I'm not an expert in the field of lucid dreams, but I can offer my opinions. Lucid dreams seem to come in two categories. The first type of lucid dream happens during the onslaught of sleep. It is possible that these experiences are actually OBEs. The second type of lucid dream occurs during REM (rapid eye movement) sleep, which researchers acknowledge as the dream state. Scientists have developed a few commercial devices that monitor the eyelids of a dreamer. When REM sleep is detected, the machine flashes a light or sends another signal to the dreamer. When the dreamer recognizes the signal, he or she can wake themselves to a fully conscious lucid dream.

Studies have shown that OBEs do not occur during REM sleep. From personal experience, I can say this much: I have experienced both OBEs and lucid dreams and have seen the difference. Lucid dream scenery seems "fake" when compared to OBE scenery. In lucid dreams I realize the scenery is "fake," and I can make the scenery dissolve, leaving me floating near my body.

What's the difference between meditation and OBE?

In some forms of meditation, the goal is to clear your mind of all thoughts, which is very similar to quiescing your mind for an OBE. Some people report accidentally leaving their bodies during meditation. Others go into a state of meditation when trying to induce an OBE, but never leave their bodies.

When I meditate, my mind becomes empty, and I go into a kind of trance that I can't explain. In this trance of meditation, I don't have any perception. I don't have dreams or hypnogogic images. It is as if the world has completely stopped, and my consciousness has been extinguished. When I come back from meditation, I have no memories.

When I induce an OBE, I don't induce nearly as deep a trance. I retain a thread of alert consciousness the whole time. Once I reach the OBE state, my consciousness becomes normal again. After the experience, I have complete memories of the experience.

How do I know if an OBE is real?

My general rule of thumb is: if you're not sure, then it was not a real OBE. A true OBE should leave you with no doubt in your mind. In a genuine OBE, you should literally feel as if you are separate from your body. It won't seem like a dream, a daydream, a visualization, or a fantasy. It will feel absolutely real.

Is consciousness clear during an OBE?

In an OBE, as in life, consciousness can be crystal clear or muddy. I've had OBEs where my consciousness was more intense than normal waking life. I've also had OBEs where my thinking was more "muddy."

What's the difference between OBEs and near death experiences?

This is how I think of it: the out-of-body experience is one typical feature of a near death experience (NDE). Typical NDEs have some other common features that aren't usually found in an OBE (although that doesn't mean they can't happen). Some of these features are gliding down a tunnel, having your life flash before your eyes, seeing a bright light, meeting dead relatives or friends, and being told it is "not your time."

Also, NDEs usually happen during times of bodily trauma. OBEs often happen from a state of perfect health.

Has anyone seen God, Jesus, or other deities during an OBE?

It is more common to see deities during NDEs than during OBEs. It's interesting to note that when this happens, it seems to be based on the person's religious convictions. Christians tend to see Christ. Buddhists tend to see The Buddha. Hindus tend to see their deities. I believe there is only one God. Perhaps certain powerful spiritual entities on the other side can appear in a form that makes the participant most comfortable. Personally, I've never seen a deity during an OBE, except for the childhood experience related in chapter 2.

When you leave your body, aren't you technically dead? Why doesn't brain damage or rigor mortis occur?

Your body does not die during an OBE. It goes into a deeply relaxed state.

Is OBE related to UFO phenomena?

Many victims of "alien abductions" describe symptoms similar to OBE phenomena. They describe tunnels, vibrations, weird sounds and sights, and total paralysis. They describe how aliens appear out of thin air beside their beds or walk through walls. Victims are levitated out of bed and are pulled outside through the wall. I believe many such victims are merely misinterpreting symptoms of typical OBEs. I think a lot of "abductees" would be relieved to know the true nature of their experiences!

I must also add that not all claims of alien abduction can be dismissed as OBEs. Some UFO cases have compelling physical evidence that wouldn't be left after an OBE. OBE's don't leave burn marks on your front lawn!

Can you inhabit the body of a medium during an OBE?
Around 1903, an invalid by the name of Vincent Turvey learned how to induce OBEs to free himself from his disabled body. Spiritualism was very popular then, so Turvey started visiting seances during his OBEs. A few times he actually sent messages through the medium during the seance. In his book, *The Beginnings of Seership*, Turvey has signed testimonials from people who were present at these seances. I believe him because he had witnesses and because he was too physically ill to stage such elaborate hoaxes. I've never tried it, and I don't know of anyone who has, other than Turvey. But I believe it can be done.

Is there a such thing as astral sex?
I've read about astral sex in only a few books. The following experience is the closest I've been. I was conscious at the time, but this experience seemed to be a bit too unbelievable, so I called it a lucid dream.

03/08/83 Thu

Last night I had an interesting experience that I'd like to share. Before I went to sleep at midnight, I prayed to God. I asked to have an experience where I would reach my soulmate through a dream . . . Sometime in the middle of the night I found myself in a dreamlike state and was semiconscious. I was not in a recognizable place. I was with a woman with light hair, and I don't know if she was my soulmate or not. We got very close to each other, and just before we embraced I became conscious in the sense of a lucid dream. The intensity of the experience is what caused me to be conscious. We embraced, and at first I thought we were hugging. Then her body became less defined and started melting into mine. I was surprised, and my body started melting too! As we melted into each other, energy started shooting out in all directions with the intensity of the sun. I can't remember any more.

What do you see when you look into a mirror?
The following is an OBE where I looked into a mirror. What I saw was surprising.

12/25/85—OBE #121

. . . I stayed in bed, practicing OBE. I used the rock-my-consciousness method to loosen myself from the body, but I felt somewhat attached to it, even as I was swinging away. On one outward swing, I twisted to my left, reached out with my astral arms, grabbed onto the bed, and pulled myself completely out of my body. I paused there, crouched down on my bed, looking at the drapes on the bedroom window. Everything looked normal from that point of view.

I had been planning to try to visit CRA, and I paused to think about visiting her. I thought, "There's plenty of time for that. First, I want to experiment a little bit." My eyes were closed because of the previous two OBEs.

I paused, trying to think of a good experiment. "I know," I thought to myself," I'll try looking into a mirror!" As soon as I thought that, I felt a strange shift of consciousness and opened my eyes.

I found myself in a strange room with a mirror. I walked over to the mirror and looked at it. At first I saw my own image, but without a beard—I only had a moustache. I thought to myself how much I looked like BA (CRA's husband). My image slowly turned into BA's image, and I thought, "Hmm. Maybe I'm a counterpart of BA. But I have a beard and a moustache, and my image doesn't reflect that." I looked into the mirror again, trying to fix the image. I noticed the image wasn't smiling; it had a very serious look. So I smiled into the mirror and watched my image change.

My image changed slowly into the image of a woman I've never seen before and then slowly turned into an image of DS, smiling! (DS is a member of our discussion group.) I thought, "Whoa! That's not me. I wonder if DS is a counterpart too!" I bid DS's image farewell, and looked into the mirror and saw myself. This time I looked normal in all respects. I was smiling, and I noticed I was wearing the same clothes my body had on in bed. I thought, "Good."

I wondered whether I should visit CRA or do another experiment. I tried to think of other experiments I could do, but I lost consciousness and immediately came to in my body.

This story had an interesting aftermath. The next day, I narrated the OBE to the discussion group, and BA was there. As nearly as we could tell, BA was just getting up and dressing during my OBE. He most likely was in the bathroom looking at a mirror! Was the image I saw of him real? I'd like to think so, but I guess there's no way to tell for sure.

How long does it take to learn?

This varies from person to person. Some books claim to be able to teach you to leave your body in thirty days or less. But that depends on a lot of factors, like your belief system, how often you practice, the methods you try, and your attitudes during practice.

Some people have tried for ten years or more before having their first OBE. Others have done it on their first try. Don't be discouraged if you don't get results for several months. Everyone can learn this skill with practice and patience.

What's a typical OBE practice session like?

On a typical practice session, I will wake up naturally around 6:30 A.M. I'll get up, visit the bathroom, then drink something with caffeine. I'll stay up for about a half hour to clear my mind. I'm usually too tired at that hour, so I'll go back to bed and sleep for another sleep cycle. Around 7:30 A.M., I'll wake up naturally, stretch, and start my first attempt. After about twenty minutes of trying, I will give up, roll over, and go back to sleep.

When I wake up from that sleep cycle, I'll make my second attempt. Again, I'll keep at it for about twenty minutes before giving up. I'm usually successful on my second or third attempt. If I'm not successful by 11:30 A.M., I quit practicing.

How long does it take to induce an OBE?

Typically, it takes around fifteen to twenty minutes to induce an OBE. My fastest induction took around thirty seconds. My longest induction took more than an hour.

What's the most common mistake during practice?

The most common mistake people make is trying too hard. Many people try so hard to induce an OBE that they never reach that totally passive state of mind I mentioned in chapter 24, step 2. If you "try hard" instead of letting go, you'll never be able to quiesce your mind enough to induce an OBE.

Why do it? What is it good for?

I believe there are many good reasons to induce out-of-body experiences. It may help us prepare for the afterlife and uncover the secrets that lie beyond death's door. And that, in turn, can bring a better understanding and appreciation for life; we gain the realization that life is, after all, only temporary. After an OBE or two, there is no longer a fear of death. Also, inducing OBEs may help us develop psychic abilities. It may also help us contact departed loved ones. Perhaps in the future, we can use it to explore the far reaches of space or the depths of the oceans, or maybe to find missing children and catch criminals. Besides, it's fun.

Most important, OBEs can help us to be more spiritual. We can find our own answers instead of relying on religion, superstition, and dogma. We can explore our own inner space and discover our inner selves. Maybe we can experience our true oversoul, or superconscious self. Perhaps we may even reach Ecstasy, Satori, Nirvana, Christ-consciousness, or whatever you want to call it. Perhaps we can even experience the divine, the infinite soul, or God. The possibilities are endless.

There are still many unanswered questions about the out-of-body experience. It seems as though the more I answers I find, the more questions pop up.

EXERCISE 26
Side-to-Side Swaying

This is similar to the method described in chapter 24. Lie down with your arms by your side. Relax your body to the point where you can no longer feel your arms. As vividly as you can, imagine that your arms are stretched out perpendicular to your body (not by your side). Hold that feeling and simultaneously slow down your mind into that quiescent state mentioned in chapter 16. If you find it difficult to reach this point, your body is probably not relaxed enough. You should be so relaxed that you do not feel your physical arms at your side. Do not continue until it feels as though your arms are outstretched. Hold your mind in that quiescent state.

Then visualize that both hands are holding onto handles that are anchored. Hold that visualization until it is stable.

Next, visualize that you flex your right outstretched arm just a tiny bit, which pulls your astral body slightly toward it. This imagined movement of your astral body should start out very small, approximately one millimeter. Your physical body should not move. (If it does, start over.) Then flex your left arm, pulling your astral body back to the left.

Again, flex your right arm, then your left arm to "sway" your astral body slightly from side to side. Keep flexing your arms right-left-right-left. As you do, develop a rhythm to your swaying. Each flex should take only half a second to achieve, so a complete cycle of right, then left should take approximately one second to complete.

Continue to hold this swaying pattern for about thirty seconds (the exact amount of time isn't important), then slowly start to increase the amount of pulling. Over about four minutes, increase the amount of swaying to about six inches per side. At that point, the vibrations are likely to hit you. Ignore them and keep swaying for about ten more seconds. Then you will be free from your body. Use the side-to-side momentum to swing yourself away.

27

The Final Frontier!

I believe we all chose to be born in this physical world for a reason. Each of us came here to accomplish certain lessons or missions, and we created our physical bodies to help us accomplish those missions. Bodies are wonderful tools. Like a television set, they can be quite entertaining and we can learn a great deal by using them. But just like television, it's good to spend some time away from them, just to give ourselves a proper perspective of the "outside" world.

We are kept inside our bodies only because of psychological barriers: our beliefs, expectations, desires, defense mechanisms, and so forth. And with practice we can remove these psychological barriers. We don't need to spend *all* our time in the body. We can roam around "outside" occasionally, for fun and adventure. All we have to lose is limitation, dogma, and fear. What we have to gain is a new frontier of consciousness.

Out-of-body experiences brought a depth and spirituality to my life that I might never have known. Every day I learn and grow. My consciousness is constantly expanding. Unlike most people, I no longer fear death.

I've heard it said that you can't fully appreciate something until it's gone. Perhaps out-of-body experiences can help us to appreciate the value of life.

The universe is ever-expanding, not only physically, but also in consciousness and depth of being. I invite you all to reach into the depths of being and touch the infinite!

Bibliography

I've been collecting OBE books ever since I started having OBEs. Here is a list of every book and tape that I know of dealing primarily with OBEs. I won't claim that it's accurate or complete. This list does *not* include books on related topics such as near death experiences (NDEs), remote viewing, shamanism, and other altered states of consciousness except when referenced in the text or listed by the Library of Congress under "Astral Projection." I merely provide the list for people who want to do further research. All books in the list are "nonfiction" unless otherwise noted.

Books in English

Arguelles, Jose. *Surfers of the Zuvuya: Tales of Interdimensional Travel*. Santa Fe, NM: Bear & Co., 1988.

Ashcroft-Nowicki, Dolores. *Highways of the Mind*. Wellingborough, Northamptonshire: The Aquarian Press, 1987.

Avery, Robert. *Out of the Body Experiences*. London and New York: Regency Press, 1975.

Baker, Dr. Douglas M. *Practical Techniques of Astral Projection*. Wellingborough, Northamptonshire: The Aquarian Press, 1977.

Barton, Winifred G. *Meditation and Astral Projection*. Ottawa, Canada: Psi Science Productions, 1974.

Battersby, H. F. Prevost. *Man Outside Himself*. Secaucus, NJ: Citadel Press, 1979.

Baumann, Elwood D. *They Travel Outside Their Bodies: The Phenomenon of Astral Projection.* New York: Watts, 1980.

Bendit, L. and P. *The Etheric Body of Man.* Wheaton, Ill.: Theosophical Publishing House, 1977.

Black, David. *Ecstasy: Out of the Body Experiences.* Indianapolis and New York: Bobbs-Merrill Company, 1975.

Blackmore, Susan J. *Beyond the Body.* Chicago: Academy Chicago Publishers, 1982.

Bord, Janet. *Astral Projection.* Wellingborough, Northamptonshire: The Aquarian Press, 1973.

Bradley, Marion Zimmer. *The House Between the Worlds* (fiction). New York: Ballantine Books/Doubleday, 1981.

Brady, Michael J. *Infinite Horizons: A Psychic Experience.* Virginia Beach: Donning, 1982.

Brennen, J. H. *Astral Doorways.* New York: Samuel Weiser, Inc., 1971.

———. *The Astral Projection Workbook.* New York: Sterling Publishing Co., 1990.

Brennert, Alan. *Kindred Spirits* (fiction). New York: Tom Doherty Associates, 1984.

Conway, D. J. *Astral Love.* St. Paul: Llewellyn Publications, 1996.

———. *Flying Without a Broom.* St. Paul: Llewellyn Pub lications, 1995.

Crookall, Dr. Robert. *The Study and Practice of Astral Projection.* Secaucus, NJ: The Citadel Press, 1960.

———. *The Case-book of Astral Projection 545-746.* Secaucus, NJ: The Citadel Press, 1972.

———. *"Dreams" of High Significance.* Moradabad, India: Darshana International, 1974.

———. *Ecstasy. The Release of the Soul from the Body.* Moradabad, India: Darshana International, 1973.

———. *Events on the Threshold of the After-life.* Moradabad, India: Darshana International, 1967.

———. *The Jung-Jaffe View of Out-of-the-Body Experiences.* London: The World Fellowship Press, 1970.

———. *Life, 'A Cheat' or 'A Sacred Burden'?* Moradabad, India: Darshana International, 1976.

————. *The Mechanisms of Astral Projection*. Moradabad, India: Darshana International, 1968.

————. *More Astral Projections: Analyses of Case Histories*. Wellingborough, Northamptonshire: The Aquarian Press, 1964.

————. *Out-of-the-body Experiences—A Fourth Analysis*. Secaucus, NJ: The Citadel Press, 1970.

————. *Psychic Breathing*. Wellingborough, Northamptonshire: The Aquarian Press, 1979.

————. *The Techniques of Astral Projection*. New York: Samuel Weiser, 1964.

Couliano, Ioan P. *Out of This World: Other-Worldly Journeys from Gilgamesh to Albert Einstein*. Boston: Shambhala, 1991.

Curtiss, H. and F. *Realms of the Living Dead*. Washington D.C.: The Curtiss Philosophic Book Co., 1926.

Dane, Christopher (Eugene Olson). *Psychic Travel*. New York: Popular Library, 1974.

DeClements, Barthe. *Double Trouble*. New York: Viking Kestrel, 1987.

Denning, M. and Phillips, O. *The Llewellyn Practical Guide to Astral Projection*. St. Paul: Llewellyn Publications, 1979.

Devereux, Paul. *Shamanism and the Mystery Lines*. St. Paul: Llewellyn Publications, 1993.

————. *Spirit Paths, Shape-Shifting and Out of Body Travel*. St. Paul: Llewellyn Publications, 1993.

Doreal, Dr. M. *Astral Projection and How to Accomplish It*. Sedalia, CO: Brotherhood of the White Temple, (date unknown).

Duncan, Lois. *Stranger with My Face* (fiction). Boston: Little, Brown, 1981.

Farthing, Geoffrey. *Exploring the Great Beyond*. Wheaton, IL: The Theosophical Publishing House, 1978.

Fahy, Christopher. *Nightflyer* (fiction). New York: Jove Publications, 1982.

Fitzell, William. *American Mystic: A Journey of Crossing the Borders of Normal Experience*. New York: Lone Pine Press, 1992.

Fox, Oliver (Hugh Callaway). *Astral Projection*. Secaucus, NJ: The Citadel Press, 1962.

————. "The Pineal Doorway," *The Occult Review* 31 (April 1920).

Frost, Gavin and Yvonne. *Astral Travel*. New York: Granada Publishing, 1982.

Gabbard, G. and S. Twemlow. *With the Eyes of the Mind*. New York: Praeger Publishers, 1984.

Gibson, Sandra. *Beyond the Mind*. New York: Tower Publications, 1981.

Giletto, Michael J. *Identity, Pain, Astral Projection*. Richmond, VA: M. Giletto, 1972.

Glaskin, G.M. *A Door to Infinity: Proving the Cristos Experience*. New York: Avery Publishing Group, 1979.

Goodman, Felicitas D. *Where the Spirits Rind the Wind*. Indianapolis: Indiana University Press, 1990.

Green, Carl R. *Out-of-Body Experiences*. Hillside, NJ: Enslow, 1993.

Green, Celia. *Out-of-the-Body Experiences*. Oxford: Institute of Psychophysical Research, 1968.

Greene, Richard A. *The Handbook of Astral Projection*. Cambridge: Next Step Publications, 1979.

———. *The Handbook of Astral Power* (revised). Nashua, NH: Next Step Publications, 1987.

Greenhouse, Herbert B. *The Astral Journey*. New York: Avon Books, 1974.

Grey, Margot. *Return from Death: An Exploration of the Near-Death Experience*. Boston: Arkana, 1985.

Gurney, Myers, Podmore. *Phantasms of the Living*. New York: Kegan Paul, Trench, Trubner & Co., 1886.

Harary, Keith and P. Weintraub. *Have an Out-of Body Experience in 30 Days*. New York: St. Martin's Press, 1989.

Harary, Keith and Russell Targ. *The Mind Race*. New York: Villard Books, 1984.

Holroyd, Stuart. *Psychic Voyages*. London: Aldus Books, 1976.

———. *Mysteries of the Inner Self*. London: Aldus Books, 1978.

Hughes, Marilynn. *Odysseys of Light*. Charlottesville, VA: Hampton Roads, 1991.

Hurwood, Bernhardt J. *The Invisibles* (fiction). Greenwich, CT: Fawcett, 1971.

Irwin, H. J. *Flight of Mind: A Psychological Study of the Out-of Body Experience*. Metuchen, NJ: Scarecrow Press, 1985.

Johnson, Raynor C. *Nurslings of Immortality*. (Publisher unknown) .

King, Francis. *Astral Projection, Magic and Alchemy*. Rochester, VT: Destiny Books, 1991.

King, Francis and Stephen Skinner. *Techniques of High Magic: A Guide to Self-Empowerment*. Rochester, VT: Destiny Books, 1991.

Knight, Gareth. *Experience of the Inner Worlds*. Cheltenham, Gloucester, England: Helios Book Service, 1975.

LaBerge, Stephen. *Lucid Dreaming*. New York: Ballantine, 1985.

LaHaye, Tim F. *Life in the Afterlife*. Wheaton, IL: Tyndale House, 1980.

Larsen, Caroline. *My Travels in the Spirit World*. (Publisher unknown).

Leadbeater, Charles W. *The Astral Plane*. Wheaton, IL: Theosophical Publishing House, 1933.

Leonard, Gladys Osborn. *My Life in Two Worlds*.

Lewis, David H. *Astral Projection*. Published by the author, 1980.

Llewellyn Editorial staff. *The Truth about Astral Projection*. St. Paul: Llewellyn Publications, 1983.

MacGregor-Mathers. *Astral Projection, Ritual Magic, and Alchemy*. Rochester, VT: Destiny Books, 1987.

Martin, Anthony. *Understanding Astral Projection*. Wellingborough, Northamptonshire: The Aquarian Press, 1980.

———. *The Theory and Practice of Astral Projection*. Wellingborough, Northamptonshire: The Aquarian Press, 1980.

Martin, Stephen Hawley. *Out of Body, Into Mind: A Metaphysical Adventure*. Richmond, VA: The Oaklea Press, 1995.

Matson, Archie. *The Waiting World: or, What Happens at Death*. New York: Harper & Row, 1975.

McMoneagle, Joseph. *Mind Trek*. Charlottesville, VA: Hampton Roads, 1993.

Mendoza, Carlos (Carlos Romolu). *Earth Refugees of the Aquarian Age*. (Publisher unknown), 1982.

Mitchell, Janet Lee. *Out-of-Body Experiences*. Willingborough, Northamptonshire: Turnstone Press, 1981.

Monroe, Robert A. *Journeys Out of the Body*. Garden City: Anchor Press/Doubleday, 1971.

———. *Far Journeys*. Garden City: Doubleday, 1985.

———. *Ultimate Journey*. Garden City: Doubleday, 1994.

Morgan, Keith. *Easy Astral Projection*. London: Pentacle Enterprises, 1992.

Morimutsu, Phil. *The Seeker*. Minneapolis: Eckankar, 1992.

Moser, Robert (Bob). *Mental and Astral Projection*. Cottonwood, AZ: Esoteric Publications, 1974.

Muldoon, Sylvan. *The Case for Astral Projection*. Chicago: The Aries Press, 1936.

Muldoon, Sylvan and H. Carrington. *The Projection of the Astral Body*. New York: Samuel Weiser, 1929.

———. *The Phenomena of Astral Projection*. New York: Samuel Weiser, 1951.

Mulvin, Jerry. *Out-of-Body Exploration*. Marina del Rey, CA: Divine Science of Light and Sound, 1986.

———. *Through the Vortex*. Marina del Rey, CA: Divine Science of Light and Sound, 1991.

Ophiel (Edward Peach). *The Art and Practice of Astral Projection*. New York: Samuel Weiser, 1961.

Owen, Robert. *Footfalls on the Boundary of Another World*. Philadelphia: J. B. Lippincott Co., 1860.

Palwick, Susan. *Flying in Place* (fiction). New York: TOR (Tom Doherty Associates), 1992.

Panchadasi, Swami. *The Astral World: Its Scenes, Dwellers, and Phenomena*. Wheaton, IL: Theosophical Publishing House.

Parker, Vincent M. "Vibes." Vincent Parker, 1994.

Perkins, John M. *Psychonavigation: Techniques for Travel Beyond Time*. Rochester, VT: Destiny Books, 1990.

Powell, Arthur Edward. *The Astral Body*. Wheaton, IL: Theosophical Publishing House, 1927.

———. *The Etheric Double*. Wheaton, IL: Theosophical Publishing House, 1927.

Prabhupada, Swami. *Easy Journey to Other Planets*. Publisher unknown, 1970.

Richards, Steve. *The Traveller's Guide to the Astral Plane*. Wellingborough, Northamptonshire: Aquarian Press, 1983.

Richelieu, Peter. *A Soul's Journey*. Wellingborough, Northamptonshire: Aquarian Press, 1953.

Out of Body Experiences

Roads, Michael J. *Into a Timeless Realm*. Tiburon, CA: H. J. Kramer, 1995.

———. *Journey Into Oneness*. Tiburon, CA: H. J. Kramer, 1994.

Rogo, D. Scott. *Leaving the Body*. Englewood Cliffs, NJ: Prentice-Hall, 1983.

———. *Mind Beyond the Body*. New York: Penguin, 1978.

Scott, Mary. *Science and Subtle Bodies: Towards a Clarification of Issues*. London: College of Psychic Studies, 1975.

Sculthorp, Fredrick C. *More about the Spirit World*. London: The Greater World Assoc., 1975.

Sewall, May Wright. *Neither Dead Nor Sleeping*. (Publisher unknown).

Shay, J. M. *Out of Body Consciousness*. Pittsburgh, NY: We are One, 1972.

Shirley, Ralph. *The Mystery of the Human Double; The Case for Astral Projection*. New York: University Books, 1965.

Smith, Suzy. *The Enigma of Out-of-Body Travel*. New York: Signet, 1965.

———. *Out-of-body Experiences for the Millions*. Los Angeles: Sherbourne Press, 1968.

Society of Metaphysicians. *An Introduction to the Study of Astral Projection*. Hastings, England: Society of Metaphysicians, 1977.

Stack, Rick. *Out-of-Body Adventures: 30 Days to the Most Exciting Experience of Your Life*. Chicago/New York: Contemporary Books, 1988.

Steiger, Brad. *Astral Projection*. Rockport, MA: Para Research, Inc., 1982.

———. *In My Soul I Am Free*. Minneapolis: Eckankar. 1968.

———. *The Mind Travellers*. New York: Award Books, 1968.

———. *Other Worlds, Other Universes: Playing the Reality Game*. Garden City, NY: Doubleday, 1975.

Studer, Jack J. *Treasures of the Psychic Realm*. Marina del Rey, CA: DeVorss & Company, 1976.

Sutphen, Dick and Trenna. *Astral Projection: Hypnosis album* (Cassettes). Scottsdale, AZ: Valley of the Sun Publishing, 1980.

Swann, Ingo. *To Kiss Earth Goodbye*. New York: Dell Publishing, 1975.

Time-Life (Editors of). *Psychic Voyages*. Richmond, VA: Time-Life Books, 1987.

Tart, Charles T. *Altered States of Consciousness*. Garden City, NY: Anchor/Doubleday, 1969.

———. *Out of the Body Experience* (sound recording). Big Sur Recordings, 1968.

Taylor, Albert. *Soul Traveler*. Covina, CA: Verity Press, 1996.

Travis, Steve. *From Out of the Blue: A Spiritual Adventure*. West Chester, PA: Whitford Press, 1990.

Turvey, Vincent. *The Beginnings of Seership*. New Hyde Park, NY: University Books, 1969.

Twitchell, Paul. *Eckankar*. New York: Lancer Books, 1969.

———. *Tiger's Fang*. Minneapolis: Eckankar.

VanDam, Vee A. K. *The Psychic Explorer*. London: Skoob Books, 1986.

Walker, Benjamin. *Beyond the Body*. Boston: Routledge & Kegan Paul, 1974.

Wake, Wilma. *Beyond the Body*. New York: Dorchester Publishing, 1979.

Willson, Terrill. *How I Learned Soul Travel*. Minneapolis: Eckankar, 1987.

YRAM (Marcel Louis Forhan). *Practical Astral Projection*. New York: Samuel Weiser, 1972.

Zaleski, Carol. *Otherworld Journeys*. New York: Oxford University Press, 1987.

OBE Books in Other Languages

Bourgine, Jerome. *Le voyage Astral: Enquete Sur les Voyages Hors du Corps*. Monaco: Editions du Rocher, 1993.

Bun Ninket. *Khomun Prachak Tai Laeo Koet*. Chiang Mai: Sun Khomun Prachak Tai Laeo.

Fabricius, Johannes. *Dodsoplevelsens Psykologi*. Kobenhavn: Rhodos, 1972.

Fischer, Reinhard. *Raumfahrt der Seele*. Freiburg, Germany: Verlag Hermann Bauer, 1975.

Guesne, Jeanne. *Le Grand Passage: Mes Experiences de Dedoublement*. Paris, France: Courrier du Livre, 1978.

Lancelin, Charles. *Methode de Dedoublement Personnel*. Paris, France: Henri Durville.

Lancelin, Charles. *La vie Posthume; Recherches Experimentales D'apres les Plus Recentes Donnees de la Physique, de la Psycho-Physiologie et de la Psychologie Experimentale.* Paris, France: Henri Durville, 1922.

Nemere, Istvan. *Kilephetsz Testedbol: A Spiritisztak Titkai.* Budapest: Libroservo, 1991.

Roca, Muntanola J. *Viaje d Antiuniverso: El Viaje Astral: Parapsicologia, Esoterismo, Metafisica.* Barcelona, Spain: Editorial Alas, 1974.

Thonhthiu Suwannathat. *Tai Laeo Pai Nai.* Kotho: Kongthun Lok Thip, 1988.

'Ubayd, Ra'uf Sadiq. *Zawahir Al-khuruj Min Al-jasad, Adil-latuha, Dalalatuha.* (Publisher unknown), 1974.

Waelti, Ernst R. *Der Dritte Kreis des Wissens: Ausserkorperliche Erfahrungen, Eine Mystik der Naturwissenschaft.* Interlaken, Germany: Ansata-Verlag, 1983.

About the Author

Robert Peterson is a computer programmer. He lives in Minneapolis. Visit him at *www.robertpeterson.org*.